The
Shopkeeper's
Home

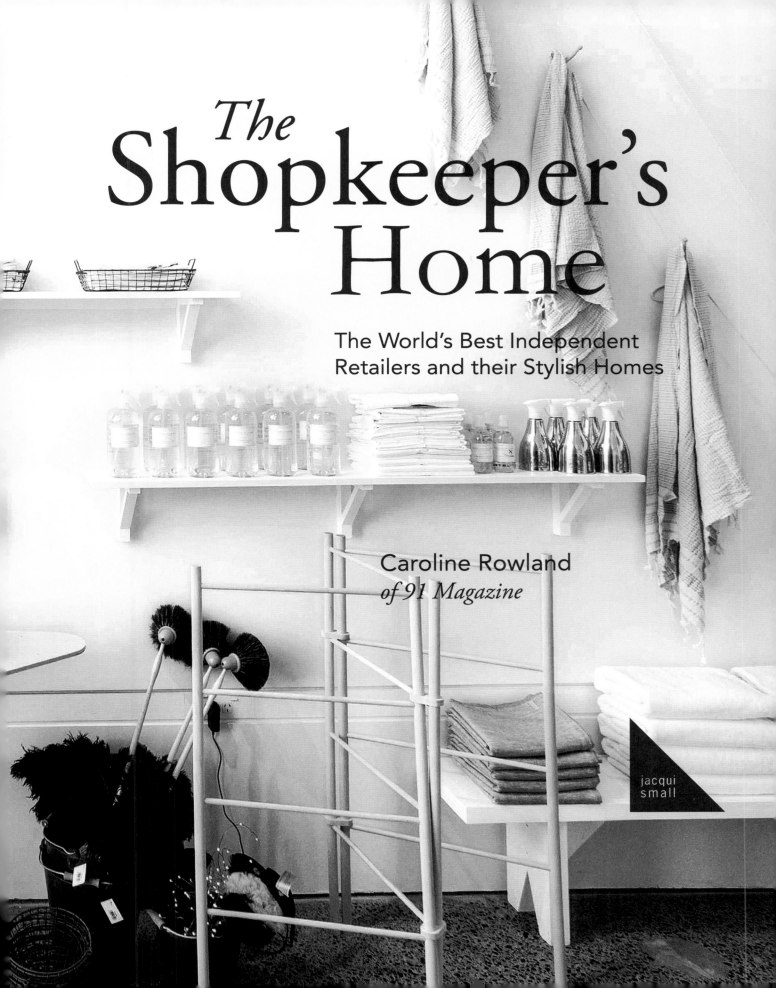

The Shopkeeper's Home

The World's Best Independent Retailers and their Stylish Homes

Caroline Rowland
of 91 Magazine

jacqui
small

For Ruby x

First published in 2015 by
Jacqui Small LLP
An imprint of Aurum Press
74–77 White Lion Street
London N1 9PF

Publisher: Jacqui Small
Commissioning Editor/Project Editor: Joanna Copestick
Managing Editor: Emma Heyworth-Dunn
Senior Designer: Rachel Cross
Production: Maeve Healy

ISBN: 9 781 909 34290 3

A catalogue record for this book is available
from the British Library.

2017 2016 2015
10 9 8 7 6 5 4 3 2 1

Printed in China

Contents

HOW TO USE THIS BOOK

Within these pages you will discover some of the world's most beautiful shop interiors, plus the stunning homes of the shopkeepers who own them. The first half of the book is filled with decorating ideas from both the stores and the homes that you can incorporate into your own home interior – how to capture a style, great tips for your walls, floors and furniture, and unusual, inventive ideas for display and storage.

Whether you prefer vintage-style homes, cool, contemporary spaces or an industrial aesthetic, there are plenty of ideas here to get you thinking creatively about your own space.

The second half of the book profiles each location and shop owner, really delving into their creative concepts and find out more about how they've decorated and styled both their retail and residential spaces and how one may have influenced the other.

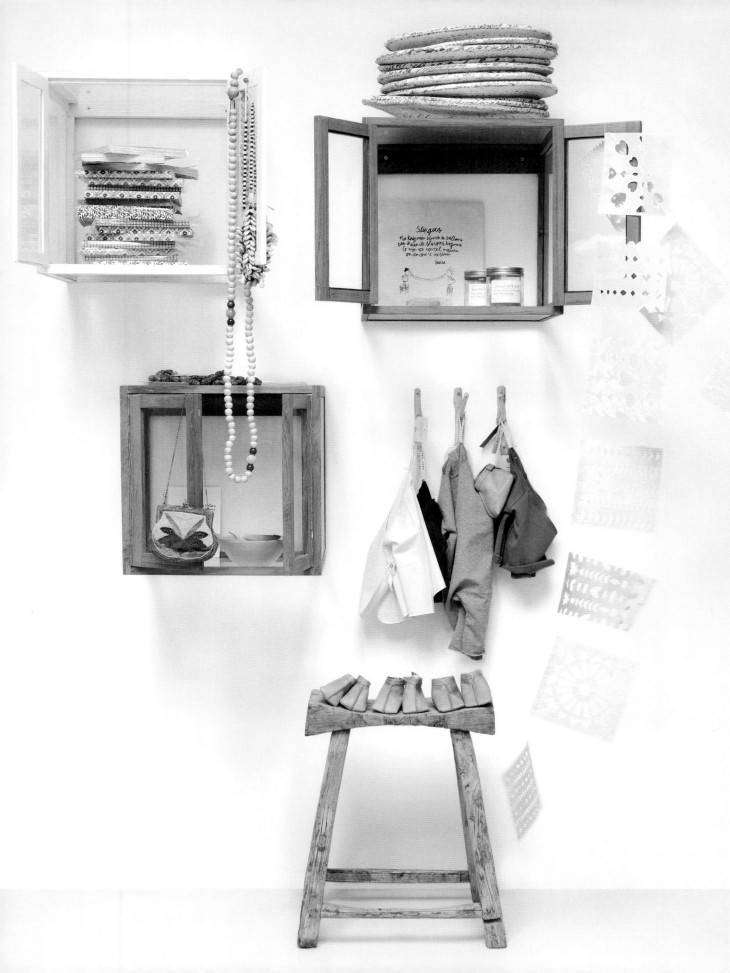

decorating ideas

STEPPING INSIDE A BEAUTIFUL SHOP OFTEN SETS THE HEART AFLUTTER – THE ANTICIPATION OF WHAT YOU MIGHT FIND, FOLLOWED BY THE LOVELY BUZZ OF RETAIL THERAPY. BUT ABOVE ALL, IT IS A CHANCE TO GATHER STYLE INSPIRATION FROM THE SHOP SURROUNDINGS AS YOU EXPLORE EACH AND EVERY CORNER.

Whether inspiration comes from how the owners have utilized a converted space, their choice of floor and wall coverings or clever solutions for displaying their goods, there are lots of great ideas that can be gathered and applied to your home interior.

Shopkeepers whose style credentials shine from their store shelves are sure to have translated this talent for decor to their own homes too, so in this section we break down the various aspects of decorating and styling, and take tips from the professionals' retail and personal spaces.

Capturing a Style

Industrial or rustic, retro or modern, the style of your home interior is up to you. Try to pinpoint a style you love and adapt it to your space. In a contemporary home you could soften hard edges with vintage styling or, in a rustic space, add in highlights of vintage or mid-century furniture to create an interesting contrast.

Most shops have a distinct aesthetic – either because of the design passion of the shop owner or their knowledge of the market, or both. When you step inside a store, you quickly become aware of the types of objects sold there. Along with some lovely purchases, you can also take away some great ideas for styling your home.

Once you know the style you want to create, look at how your space can contribute to this. Is it best to keep all walls and floors neutral, or do you want to introduce patterned wallpaper to complement plainer furnishings? Think about the use of colour too.

There are no rules when it comes to capturing a style, but it is worth taking time to consider elements such as furniture, textiles, lighting and decorative items to ensure your look is coherent, not confused.

Left Harvest & Co. in Amsterdam stocks a collection of vintage industrial furniture, lighting and decorative items. The merchandise perfectly suits the building – formerly a plumbing company – and the raw interior has concrete and wooden flooring, exposed pipework and factory lighting.

Top left *The Vintage Factory shop (page 134) takes inspiration from the 1950s, with candy colours and a checkerboard floor.* **Top right** *Vintage furniture mixes with delicate designer lighting in the home of Emily Chalmers, owner of Caravan (page 104), all set against a fresh white backdrop.* **Bottom left** *The Dusty Deco shop (page 112) displays retro-cool furniture alongside contemporary art, resulting in an edgy vintage look for this Stockholm warehouse space.* **Bottom right** *Natural materials and a pared-back colour palette create a serene vibe in Amsterdam-based Sukha.*

In this sitting area in Emily Chalmers's home, mid-century furniture has been given a quirky update with vintage floral fabric to soften the clean lines of the room. The space has an overall feel of eclectic laid-back style – an exposed brick wall forms a centrepiece, while stacks of books and vintage paintings are casually dotted around. If vintage is your thing, think about the various looks that can be achieved with your second-hand finds.

In store at Summer Camp (page 88), which is a converted petrol station, the curation and display of every product convey the owner's love of the great outdoors. The white walls and concrete floor, a throwback to the building's original incarnation, offer a simple backdrop against which a charming collection of sporting memorabilia and outdoor living paraphernalia are beautifully displayed so they are easy to appreciate.

Floors and Walls

The surfaces within your space are a canvas on which to build upon. Shops are great places for pilfering ideas as they often have to be clever about how to utilize walls and floors in their displays, either by making a feature of them or paring them back.

floors

Flooring greatly contributes to the overall look of a room. You may be lucky and have been blessed with beautiful original floorboards or parquet in your home, so be sure to emphasis this feature. Otherwise there are many great replica options on the market, or you could try reclaimed wood. Old boards can be left bare to let the patina through, or painted for a fresh look.

As shop floors tend to experience a high level of wear and tear, many go for a durable material such as concrete. Californian shop Summer Camp (page 88)has kept its converted gas station's raw concrete floor, while at Rare Device (page 168) the floor is painted – a good option for period as well as contemporary homes.

Left *Enormous Persian rugs have been layered up over the barn floor at UK vintage store Home Barn (page 126).*

Opposite left *Polished concrete is a hard-wearing yet super-stylish alternative to wooden floors and works in many different styles of interior.*

Opposite right *Make a feature of your staircase by wallpapering the risers in a colourful pattern.*

Take inspiration from more experimental flooring in shops, and paint or stencil a design or phrase onto wood, concrete or tiles. This is a unique way to add colour and fun, which can also be personalized, if desired. Make a feature of your stairs by pasting patterned wallpaper, adding decals or painting coordinating colours on the risers.

If you prefer comfort underfoot, of course carpet or rugs are the obvious option. They come in a vast array of price ranges, so set your budget and do your research to find the best possible quality you can afford. Look out for vintage rugs at flea markets, as these will have lots of character and you can always have them cleaned, if need be. Go for kilim rugs in beautiful colours for a traditional look or make a statement with a bold modern design. Layering rugs is a great way of creating a laid-back, boho look – choose a style and layer a few in different colours and sizes. Persian rugs or animal skins work well for this.

FLOORING SOLUTIONS

Nowadays floors don't have to be made only of wood or laid with woollen carpet. Here are some cool alternatives.

- Layering rugs over an existing wooden floor creates a sense of enclosure and some visual variety. Try mixing up the colours for even more impact.

- Polished concrete is inexpensive compared to stripped and waxed or varnished wooden floorboards. It also offers a neutral but stylish surface and works in many different styles of home.

- Create a focal point in hallways and landings by painting or wallpapering stair risers in a colourful pattern if you have a neutral decorative scheme.

- There are lots of great stencil designs around these days, and they are not just reserved for walls. Create a patterned floor or apply a bold design centrally onto floorboards or concrete as a focal point.

- Painted wooden floors are hard to beat for durability and flexibility. A glossy white floor will cheer up the darkest of interiors and can be touched up easily after family gatherings or careless pets.

walls

When it comes to the walls in your home, the possibilities are endless. Shops are often more innovative when it comes to coverings, display and features, so there are lots of great ideas you can steal from both the shops and the owners' homes.

Add texture by utilizing the building's existing features, such as interior brick walls, or by installing wood panelling. Choose weathered, reclaimed wood for a rustic cabin feel, or paint panels white for a fresher, beach-house vibe. Brickwork and textured plaster, either painted or left bare create interest.

Above Cladding a wall in reclaimed wood creates an eye-catching feature that is warm and rustic. Clever lighting will stop the area from looking too dark.

Opposite Rough exposed brick can even look great in a mid-century home. Here it contrasts with a contemporary wood-burning stove and a smooth, polished concrete floor.

BEAUTIFUL WALLS

With wallpaper here to stay and a return to industrial-style raw walls, there are many choices to make when planning which kind of surface to choose.

• Clad walls in wood salvaged from scaffolding boards, wooden pallets or reclaimed floors. Alternatively, many new wallpaper designs are available in weather-beaten or distressed wood.

• The industrial aesthetic is very much on trend and is relatively simple to achieve. Either leave bare plaster exposed for a textured look or chip it off to reveal delightfully patinated brickwork beneath.

• Painted tongue-and-groove panelling never goes out of vogue and works really well in rustic settings or in outdoor cabins used for work.

• Experiment with statement walls by papering one wall in a dramatic or quirky wallpaper and keep the others in a plain painted colour.

• Pegboard is a versatile way of introducing a display space along a single wall.

Furniture

The world is your oyster when it comes to furniture. Flea-market finds, design classics or repurposed one-offs, all contribute to establishing your interior look. Work out what really appeals to you and suits your space before taking the time to hunt down some perfect pieces for a good mix.

repurposing

Shop owners are continually on the lookout for great pieces of furniture, either to sell, to use as display units or to furnish their own homes. By looking at objects with a fresh eye, you can start to envisage new ways of repurposing items or breathing new life into them. For example, flea markets are rife with old chairs, but often they are single dining seats or look tired and tattered. Barter for a great price, then give them a simple lick of paint or re-cover the seat pads in new fabric, and mismatch them with other great seating. Stick to a complementary colour palette so the mixture of chair styles ties together effortlessly.

Of course armchairs or sofas can also be updated with new upholstery. Look at the shape and scale of the piece first. If you like it, then consider the condition and whether it is suitable for re-covering. Car boot sales and house clearances are great places to pick up a budget-busting piece of furniture, then,

***Right** With so many wonderful chair designs around, don't feel obliged to stick with only one for your dining table. Have one of each of your favourite styles to create a mismatched look.*

DIFFERENT STYLES AND ERAS

With so many furniture styles to choose from, it's worth identifying your preferences while simultaneously observing what will work best in your living areas.

- Look out for clever folding furniture if your space is limited. Vintage drop-leaf tables are perfect for tiny dining nooks, or even as a work desk, which can be folded down when not in use.

- Stacking stools or folding chairs are useful too – search for retro school seating in wood, metal or moulded plastic for a utilitarian look, or modern versions designed specifically for small spaces.

- Large, open-plan rooms lend themselves to generously proportioned pieces, which won't get lost in the space. Chunky leather club chairs and farmhouse-style furniture have a solidness to them that will create a presence in a large room.

- In a large space, be bold and add fun elements like a hanging cocoon chair or a hammock, and use furniture to separate an open living space into zones.

simply choose your covering. Perhaps you have a favourite piece of vintage fabric you've been saving, or you want to match it to your current colour scheme. Or think outside the box and use unusual materials; old grain sacks are perfect for a hard-wearing surface or you could perhaps patchwork your children's old clothes for a nostalgic touch.

Items not originally intended as home furnishings are often the most interesting. Lynda Gardener, owner of Empire Vintage in Melbourne (page 138), uses an old haberdashery display unit as a kitchen island, while metal school lockers house her china, glassware and linens. Check out how shops incorporate repurposed pieces into their store design, as these can often be translated into the home. A sewing machine table could be a great hallway console, an old workshop bench would make a sturdy feature in a large kitchen, or, you could construct a table from wooden pallets, a clever way to make furniture for next to nothing.

Consider repurposing industrial pieces originally intended for factories and check out salvage yards for oversized items that will fill a big expanse. Wooden shutters make a great feature in a living space, either fixed to the windows, leaned against a wall or as a space divider. Inheritance owner Michael Andrews (page 146) has used plinths to display objects. Also consider a full-height ladder propped against the wall in an open-plan kitchen/living room.

Left *Industrial metal chairs make great companions to a dining table or a work desk – the more patina the better.*

Opposite *Old crates and pallets are usually cheap to buy and can be easily repurposed into fabulous furniture such as this large table in the Amsterdam store, Sukha.*

TEN GREAT FURNITURE IDEAS

Think out of the box when it comes to furniture. Rooms are always more appealing and welcoming when furnished with innovative, repurposed or carefully curated pieces that mix or meld with one another rather than obviously adhering to a matchy-matchy formula or colour palette.

1. A woodworker's bench repurposed as a display table **2.** This 1950s cabinet stores wool, at a glance. **3.** Battered leather chairs are perfect for an industrial setting. **4.** Bring a simple sofa to life with a pile of soft, textural cushions. **5.** Combine pieces of retro 1950s furniture for a vintage feel. **6.** Retro cafe chairs are effortlessly stylish combined with a pallet table. **7.** An 'ostrich feet' table is glamorous and elegant. **8.** Painted corner tables make great focal points. **9.** Painted rattan is comfortable and comforting. **10.** Reclaimed benches are practical and welcoming additions to kitchens, dining spaces and bedrooms.

Lighting

The illumination of your home should never be boring.
Gather unique and stylish ideas from shop owners
who make it their mission to correctly light their stores
and homes, while integrating it into the decor.

Daybed
Jij mag altijd
met je hoofd vol wens
bij mij komen liggen
hier ben je vrij
want ik trek geen grens
tussen dag en nacht
dromen mag
altijd bij mij
ook overdag

Sukha

Lighting is an important part of any decorating scheme, not only in terms of creating an ambience, but the style and fittings you choose are critical to tying a look together or potentially standing out as one of the main features in a room.

There are so many options available, from factory-style enamel pendants and pretty fabric shades to unusual wall lights and quirky lamps. Industrial lighting is particularly popular at the moment and can be found in a variety of colours, finishes and sizes. Giant pendant shades create impact, while freestanding studio-style lights are a hip alternative to standard floor lamps. Smaller enamel shades look great grouped together in a set of three, above a dining table or kitchen island, for example.

In fact, grouping pendant lighting works particularly well when using the rule of three.

Top left Repurpose wire and wicker baskets as lampshades and consider grouping them together for an unusual arrangement.

Top right Enamel factory shades work in many different décor styles and are classically stylish without overpowering the space.

Right Simple bare bulbs grouped in threes, hung from coloured wires, create a contemporary look that is inspired by vintage industrial style.

Opposite Even in a pared-back, calm space you can still opt for a dramatic lighting statement.

Left *At Caravan (page 102), a varied collection of lighting sits in a corner of the store.*

Below Carnival lighting is a fun way to personalize your space. Spell out a word or initial, like in Oh Hello Friend.

Danni Hong of Oh Hello Friend has done this in her own bedroom (page 86) with a series of repurposed wire lampshades, positioning them in one corner of the room.

Pleasingly unexpected, this is an interesting way to light a desk or reading area, for example. Or, consider breaking the rule of three, and cluster numerous shades together. This idea would work well in a large room with high ceilings, where you could vary the length of the cables, sizes and colours of the shades for a bright and fun feature.

Chandeliers are the antithesis of utilitarian lighting, adding sparkle and glamour to any room, but try to find something a little out of the ordinary. Search for truly magnificent vintage versions, or track down independent designers making contemporary alternatives. Caravan owner Emily Chalmers demonstrates how you can mix styles of lighting for an eclectic look. In her open-plan living area she combines an elaborate vintage chandelier, an angled task lamp and a wall-mounted cross made from coloured bulbs.

For something really unique, commission your own original piece of lighting. Take inspiration from Beam & Anchor, who have installed a large lightbox printed with their brand name (page 122),

DECORATIVE LIGHTING

Practically, we need lighting to illuminate our homes, but don't allow your light fittings to be boring or inconspicuous. Vintage, industrial, repurposed or designer — the choices are endless, so take time to select the right piece.

- In a large room with high ceilings, an oversized, statement light will create drama. A huge chandelier or an edgy contemporary piece will work well.

- Open-plan living will benefit from zoning, with help from your lighting. A trio of bare bulbs above a kitchen island, an industrial pendant light over the dining table and an Anglepoise lamp next to a reading chair will help to assign each area its tasks.

- A table lamp is essential for bedtime reading or for creating a subdued atmosphere in the living room of an evening, but don't let it fade into the background in the style stakes.

- Carnival and neon lights are really popular and are a fun way to personalize your space.

- Lots of vintage items can be repurposed into lampshades — wire baskets, old jars, tins, colanders, and jelly moulds can all be adapted, so keep your eyes peeled and your mind open for clever ideas.

- For something unique, check out lampshade-making classes so you can design and make your own.

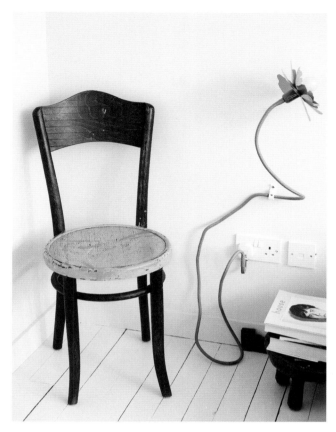

or spell out initials or a short phrase with carnival lights. These can be mounted on the wall or simply propped up for a relaxed look. These ideas can be pricey, so for a budget-friendly but unique lighting feature, think about repurposing an item into a shade. Scour flea markets for objects such as an old colander, a wire basket or glass mason jars.

Top *Bedside lighting shouldn't be boring. Look out for unusual designs like this flower-shaped lamp.*

Bottom *For more understated yet stylish bedside illumination, a simple tripod-legged lamp fits the bill.*

Above *Who says you can have only one ceiling light?! Take inspiration from Adeline Klam's Paris shop (page 216) and hang multiple lampshades in a mix of sizes, patterns and colours for a fun feature.*

Opposite *For workspace lighting, you don't necessarily need to opt for a simple desk lamp. Go bold with a dramatic pendant light above your desk.*

Textiles

There is so much scope for how to utilise fabrics in your home. They not only add a feeling of cosiness but can be used for creating interesting features and displays too. Anything from an old silk scarf to balls of yarn can become a focal point in your space.

Without textiles, we would all be living in hard, echo- prone boxes, lacking warmth and comfort. As well as creating a homey and relaxed atmosphere, textiles give you the opportunity to introduce colour and also come up with some clever ideas for decorating your walls, windows and floors.

Adding cushions and throws are the most obvious way to add texture, and of course there are endless shapes, designs and colours you could opt for. But if you want something that no one else will have on their sofa, then simply make your own – there are lots of tutorials online if you need a hand. Scour markets for vintage fabrics, or even use fabric from some old clothes. Woven and crochet blankets are really popular right now – look on Etsy or eBay for vintage versions, or find new styles by independent makers who are reinventing the craft. Make a feature of your blanket collection by folding them in a neat stack when not in use, or by storing them rolled up in a large basket.

Floor rugs are great on hard surfaces, not only for comfort underfoot, but also for injecting colour or pattern into a room. But rugs can also be used in other ways; use small, soft sheepskins on chairs or stools for an extra touch of luxury. Alternatively, why not hang a large patterned rug on a wall for a tactile piece of art?

For something less dominating, but similarly textured, follow the trend for woven wall hangings,

Left Don't pack away favourite kids clothing that they have grown out of. Hang them in the children's room for a nostalgic, colourful display. Look out for cute clothes hangers and hooks to complement them.

Opposite Rugs aren't just for floors. Hang a single rug or a collection vertically for a tactile wall feature.

Left For an alternative to cushions, why not use small sheepskin rugs on stools like Atomic Garden owner Jamie has done in her kitchen?

Opposite Vintage handbags and clothing are often simply too beautiful to be stored in cupboards awaiting their next outing, but by hanging your favourites on the wall, you can admire them every day.

which have seen a comeback recently. Lots of textile artists are creating contemporary pieces using current colour palettes that will create a talking point in your space. Or, if you're a crafty type, look into making your own – you can find affordable looms online to get you started.

If you do enjoy crafts, then don't forget that the materials themselves can look lovely on display. Baskets or zinc buckets filled with balls of yarn not only add colour, but also reflect part of your personality into your living space. Fabric collections look wonderful stacked on shelves or in glass-fronted cabinets too. It also means your stash is organised and easily accessed.

Think about how you can repurpose textiles too. Visit flea markets and antique shops and look out for vintage silk scarves and handkerchiefs – these can be bought cheaply and, once you've gathered a few, you could stitch them together into a curtain or a blind.

FIXING A STYLE WITH TEXTILES

Textiles can be hugely influential when putting together a decorative scheme. Sometimes a particular fabric, a motif or a texture will inspire an entire room scheme.

- The texture of the fabrics you incorporate will greatly contribute to the aesthetic of the space. Luxurious velvets and silks mix well with a rustic backdrop such as an exposed brick or bare plaster wall for a rough luxe look. On the other hand, chunky knits and crochet blankets have a homespun feel, perfect for a cosy cottage vibe.

- Collect vintage fabrics and use them to craft your own unique soft furnishings. Make a curtain from silk scarves, or mismatched cushion covers in contrasting colours and patterns.

- Introduce contemporary geometrics and bold Aztec prints subtly by means of a cushion or two, or make a statement with a chevron rug.

- Textiles are one of the easiest ways to introduce colour in a flexible way. If you prefer your walls and floors simple, then add pops of colour via throws, curtains or even a favourite dress hung on the wall.

Above *The white colour palette inside Sukha is broken up only by the natural shades of wood and the rich green colours of indoor plants.*

Opposite left *A hammock is a must for enjoying such a calm, relaxing space.* **Opposite right** *Introduce colour subtly via ceramics and kitchenware in pale pastel tones.*

Colour Stories

Colour is hugely important in the home and, if so inclined, you can make one shade the dominant decorating theme. There's a fine balance between getting it right and overdoing it, but neutral backdrops are helpful in allowing your favourite hue to take centre stage.

white/neutral

Sukha in Amsterdam is a calming oasis of pale, neutral colours located in a warehouse space in the heart of the city. Step inside the store, and you will instantly feel the need to put your feet up and relax.

The design aesthetic is based around the store's sustainable product range – everything, whether furniture, accessories or even clothes, is made from from natural materials such as wood, wool, linen or cotton. As a result the colour palette is neutral – white, cream and grey dominate – with occasional colour provided by ceramics or flowers.

Walls and floors have been kept pure white, but the addition of rustic wood, cosy textiles and indoor plants stops the space from looking stark or cold.

Bold, graphic artwork on the walls also helps to give the composed space a subtle edge, while layered textures prevent the space from feeling too cold. Shell chandeliers, bamboo matting and tree trunk banners further soften this clean, white space.

blues

Often a homeowner's favourite colour is obvious from their living space, as they are naturally drawn to items of a certain shade when shopping. But when styling your space with your favourite hue, it is essential that you pitch it just right. Blue has become a signature shade for Sew Over It owner Lisa Comfort, both in her craft cafe and at home. In store, she has opted for bright turquoise pops of colour against white walls and furniture, choosing to pick out only certain pieces to paint – chairs, some shelves and drawer handles – as well as a large, stencilled quote on one wall, which creates a bold focal point.

At home, Lisa has created a more serene space, but still uses lots of her beloved blue. Her technique has been to keep a mostly neutral backdrop, and add a spectrum of blues with accessories such as cushions, throws, vases and mirrors. The variety of shades are tied together by the patterned rug, which incorporates all the blues from turquoise through to royal blue. The mixture of patterned and plain textiles stops the room looking like a block of colour, while the bright accent of the mirror contrasts perfectly with the navy blue of the fireplace.

Above left *Lisa Comfort, proprietor of London's Sew Over It, introduced her signature blue shade by painting chairs and shelves as well as an inspiring quote on the wall.*

Above right *The blue-painted wall makes for a colourful backdrop to Lisa's display of sewing notions in glass jars, as the bright shade can be seen through the glass.*

Opposite *Lisa's love of blue translates to her own home, where she mixes a spectrum of shades in the living area. The patchwork-style rug pulls together the various patterns and blue tones for a coherent look.*

yellow

The owner of Oh Hello Friend, Danni Hong, lives in the sunshine state of California, so it is no surprise that she's a fan of yellow. Her love affair with this bright colour is evident throughout her home, but at the same time it is not overdone. Yellow can be the hardest of all colours to succeed with in decorating, at least on the walls. Too often yellow can be overstimulating, especially if used in sharp tones in living spaces. It often works far better as an accent colour on furnishings or on decorative accessories such as vases or pitchers.

Danni has injected shots of the colour into her home by dotting around yellow accessories, from textiles and embroidered sunflower pictures to kitchenware and a cute bedside alarm clock. Although it is a colour that many are understandably nervous of using in the home,

she proves it can be a great choice that coordinates with many colour palettes, including neutral tones, primary hues and pastel shades.

In order for the yellow to shine through but not dominate, Danni has kept her walls a crisp white and created interest using colour and pattern through her choice of furniture, textiles and artwork. As well as the obvious ways of adding colour, such as with cushions and rugs, Danni has introduced yellow via some quite unexpected items, such as the battery- operated scooter in the living room, and the set of yellow arrows by the fireplace. Even yellow-headed matchsticks feature on the coffee table, and bunches of bright, ball-shaped billy buttons appear sporadically around the house.

While some might see yellow as a bold choice in the home, Danni has used it in a subtle and fun way, bringing small splashes of sunshine to every corner of her LA home.

If you opt for using yellow at home, take some cues from Danni and include a mix of bright and subtle shades, keeping larger areas of colour quite muted to avoid the colour dominating the space and detracting from everything else in a room.

Top left and Opposite below *Danni is always drawn to vintage finds in her beloved yellow; an easy shade to spot when rummaging at flea markets and thrift stores.*

Above *Dried flowers in yellow make a pleasing display in a wire holder in Danni's living room.*

Opposite top *The yellow and white rug in Danni's living room is a statement piece, instantly indicating her favourite colour, which is then picked out in accessories around the room too.*

Collecting/Curating

Incorporating large or even small collections into your home decor can be tricky. Carefully consider your display options, as well as what ties the collection together, such as colour, form or theme. This will let your favourite finds shine as they should.

Collections often happen by accident. You find yourself drawn to a certain item every time you are out shopping, and slowly a collection amasses. Your passion could be old books, vintage china or buttons; whatever you collect, you will want to display your treasured finds proudly, rather than hiding them away. That said, you don't want your home to resemble a museum, so think about how you curate your collection so it becomes key to your scheme.

Very small items are tricky to display, so look out for vintage printer trays, which can be mounted on the wall and filled with tiny trinkets. If you collect buttons or beads, use a series of uniform glass jars and colour-code your collection. Lined up on a shelf, everything will look tidy, organized and the jars will show off what's inside.

Pigeon-hole shelving is great for displaying small to medium-sized objects, although they all need to be of a similar size. Susan Cropper of Loop, in London, has used some for her collection of yarn in the store. She has employed the colour-coding technique too, making a simple display of yarn particularly pleasing (page 212).

The main thing is to create some sort of uniformity within your collection. With objects of the same size, such as plates or teacups, create linear or grid formations, either on shelving or on the wall. With items of varying sizes but alike in form, you can create simple vignettes. The grouping of lots of similar objects makes for an eye-catching display.

Collections of art prints or photography could be tied together either by sticking to one theme – natural history, for example, or perhaps, one particular artist's work that you love, with clear similarities of style – or by keeping the framing all the same. Pictures of different sizes and shapes are best hung in an asymmetric arrangement, however

ORGANIZING COLLECTIONS

Depending on your collections, there are different ways to make the most of how you display them. If you've spent the time scouring the planet for the perfect finds, then you must ensure you show them off in the best possible way.

- Using the rule of three is a balanced way to display and view items. This is useful for hanging pictures of the same size or for smaller collections of things such as teapots.

- If you have a large art collection, then group the pieces en masse for an impressive effect, especially if displayed from floor to ceiling. Keep the arrangement asymmetrical so you can fill gaps with new pieces.

- Use colour to tie your collection together. Group items of similar shades for a coherent display.

- Create interesting vignettes with your eclectic finds. Ensure you vary size, shape and height, perhaps adding in stacks of books to create platforms.

Top *If your art collection is large, stairwells are a good place for displaying lots of pieces of varying shapes and sizes together.*

Above *Collections of uniform size and form look their best when displayed symmetrically.*

Opposite *Wall-mounted shelving above a sideboard adds extra space for displaying a collection. Small items can reside on the shelves while larger items fill the sideboard surface.*

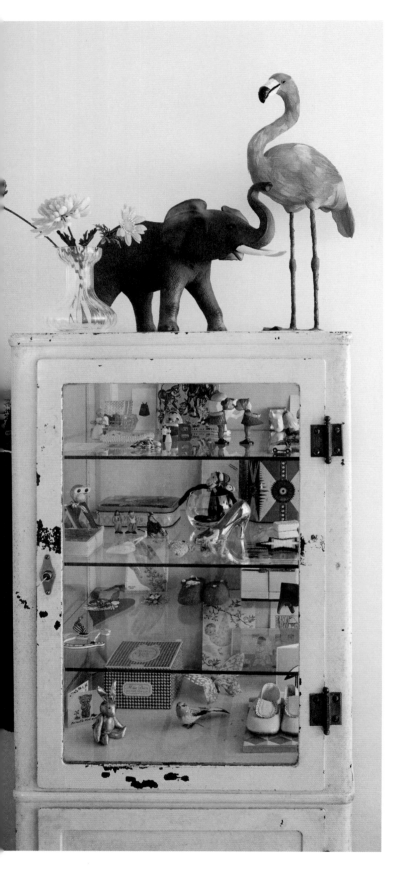

if your prints are exactly the same in dimension and frame style, a grid gallery wall will work well.

Look out for furniture or display units to house your items. Non-intrusive floating shelves allow the focus to be on your collection, or you could choose a vintage, wall-mounted shelf, which may complement the objects nicely. Glass-fronted cabinets are of course perfect for protecting items from dust, as are cloches. Both are great for more varied collections – perhaps you enjoy gathering found items but there is no particular theme. Cabinets can be filled with a variety of bits and bobs, while cloches are ideal for highlighting one or two gems. There may even already be a specific display option for whatever it is you collect. Danni of Oh Hello Friend sourced vintage rubber stamp holders for her beloved collection of rubber stamps.

Finally, think about colour. Will you group similar shades together or will it work to have a rainbow of different hues? And what backdrop will best highlight your collection? Plain white, a softer shade or a bright pop of colour? Choose something that complements your objects while still tying in with your overall decor.

Left *Look out for vintage glass-fronted cabinets for holding lots of tiny, precious items. You may find the perfect piece for your space, but if not, consider repainting and restoring a cabinet that needs some love, customizing it to suit your collection.*

Opposite *Create a cute gallery wall using your children's drawings, illustrations or postcards. Stick to one type of frame for coherence.*

Display

A top priority in any retail space and home environment, display is what makes a space truly interesting. Focus on constructing picture-perfect vignettes and think creatively in terms of using unexpected items in new ways.

on walls

Shop owners are well versed at utilizing wall space, both as a means to make the most of all surfaces available and as an interesting and exciting way to display their merchandise.

Items that aren't typically fixed to walls can turn out to make a unique display that could easily be adapted for a home setting. For example, London's Labour and Wait mounted a series of household brushes of varying shapes and sizes in store – an idea that could work well in a utility room. Not only does the display look great, but it is also a functional and accessible way to store these items. They've also used traditional hardware-store pegboards, again a practical storage solution that becomes a feature in itself. Think about spray-painting a pegboard for a contemporary update and an injection of colour.

Plates, rugs, stuffed animals and birds, even vintage sports equipment are all examples of three-dimensional elements you can try adding to your walls. If something is too large or heavy to be physically mounted, you can always just lean it against the wall, as Beam & Anchor's Jocelyn and Robert have done with a vintage surfboard in their living space. You can even use this casual approach with framed pictures or painted canvases for a relaxed, bohemian feel.

Open shelving and wall cabinets are an obvious way to display your favourite possessions. Make them into a feature by crafting your own box shelves and lining them with pretty paper, by repurposing wooden crates or by painting existing shelves in bright colours.

For an interesting, wall-based vignette, try mixing objects such as paintings or cards in a striking scene.

Left *London's Labour and Wait store has created a display of household brushes – a great idea for a utility room.*

Opposite *In a hallway, wire shelving displays a collection of globes as well as personal items and photos.*

BLACKWALL
STATION
POPLAR
ALDGATE
TOWER HILL
CANNON STREET
ALDWYCH
OXFORD STREET
PADDINGTON
PADDINGTON
BASIN

EVERYTHING'S
ALRIGHT

ways to display

Shopkeepers rely on great displays to show off their wares and, ultimately, to sell them. So, unsurprisingly, they spend a great deal of time sourcing or constructing the right furniture and fittings, and coming up with clever and stylish display ideas to use in store, many of which translate to their homes too.

Wall-mounted shelving, glass-fronted cabinets, sideboards, dressers and trolleys (wheeled carts), both industrial and retro, are all great pieces for displaying objects. Look out for unusual finds at flea markets and house clearances – they can always be repainted or updated by adding some new handles or glass, if needed. For something a little unusual, plinths or columns can create a unique feature that highlights

Top and above *At Oh Hello Friend (page 80), items have been repurposed to create fun displays. Old crates become shelving, while a muffin tin shows off cute stationery items.*

a special find. These generally work best in larger, open spaces, although Sean Scherer of Kabinett and Kammer in New York has used some in his dining room to great effect. Reclamation yards are a good place to look for these. While you're there, keep an eye out for other items that could be repurposed for display. Old ladders can be propped against or hung on a wall and used to display fabrics, shoes or plants. You could even suspend one horizontally from the ceiling and hang pots and pans from it, or wrap it in fairy lights for a pretty feature.

Hanging things from above is an interesting and space-saving technique. You could transform a piece of driftwood into a suspended shelf, or follow the revived trend for macramé and create a hanging display of plants. Decorations such as tissue paper pompoms and honeycomb balls make for a playful display while adding a splash of colour.

Always be on the lookout for quirky finds you could use to add interest to everyday items. Danni, owner of Oh Hello Friend, has used mini glass cloches and a muffin tin to display small air plants. Markets and car boot sales or garage sales are great for finding vintage silver and glassware, which can have a multitude of uses, from displaying flowers, cutlery or make-up brushes. Try using objects in ways other than what they were intended for.

Top *These house-shaped shelves are a simple DIY idea made from wood and painted or papered in bright colours. Garlands are an affordable way to add colour and fun.*

Bottom *Warehouse and loft-style spaces often have fittings you can utilize in your decor. If not, you could construct your own industrial shelving from metal piping and wood.*

TEN GREAT DISPLAY IDEAS

Good display will add a special something to a treasured collection or a grouping of similar objects. Think about ways to bring out the best in what you're putting on show. Use impact, colour or repetition, or play with height and decorative elements to create the desired effect. Above all, have fun deciding on your display.

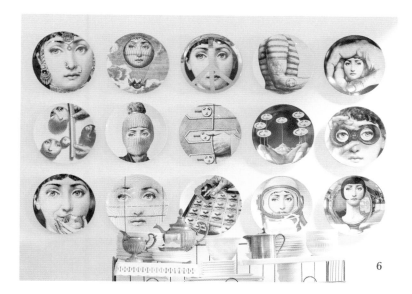

1. Pegboards are a versatile way of displaying utility items. **2.** Glass-fronted cupboards are ideal for displaying treasured kitchenalia. **3.** Group several mirrors to reflect light in a living space. **4.** Paintings leaning against a wall make an informal art installation. **5.** Differing heights create a vignette. **6.** A grid formation is perfect for items of identical shape and size. **7.** Glass cloches protect your most cherished items. **8.** Simple wooden pegs display cute children's clothes. **9.** Line wooden boxes with colourful wallpaper for a handmade look. **10.** An old suitcase displays its wares.

Storage

A tidy home lends itself to clever storage, and shop owners know this to be true for a welcoming retail space too. A large cupboard is a lifesaver for hiding away unsightly essentials, while pigeon-hole shelving holds lots, but displays your possessions proudly.

Good storage is a necessity for an organized and uncluttered home. This is something that most of us want but don't always achieve. If you arm yourself with lots of clever storage solutions, then you are more likely to utilize them and keep a clutter-free home. For those items that need to be accessible, but are best tidied away, there are many options.

Built-in cupboards and shelving can be made to

your specifications and generally take up less floor space. Jamie Kidson, co-owner of Atomic Garden, has an ingenious idea in her kitchen: shelving with shutters that can be opened up to the dining room, making the two rooms feel open-plan and sociable when needed, and separate at other times (see left). She also has cupboards above and below for tidying away unattractive kitchenware.

If you prefer freestanding furniture, which has the advantage of coming with you if you move house, then go for sideboards or dressers, which have cupboard space and display surfaces. Glass-fronted cupboards are great if you want to have your china, books or craft supplies visible for example. But if you'd prefer to conceal the contents, then add some pretty fabric to the inside of the doors, which will also give the cupboard a personalized makeover. Trolleys (wheeled carts) are another great idea if you don't mind your things being on display; choose from industrial metal, rustic wood or retro glass versions.

Left *Open shelving creates a more social feel, but shutters can be closed over when the space calls for separation. A great solution.*

Opposite *Industrial shelving can be built to suit your needs. Display treasured items proudly or use vintage containers to store small items.*

Opposite and Above *Keep your eyes peeled at flea markets for wonderful storage units like these ones. They are much more interesting visually than a standard chest of drawers, but still hold lots of possessions.*

DECORATIVE STORAGE SOLUTIONS

Make your storage solutions decorative in their own right and you will add a layer of invention and visual interest to your decorative scheme, whether you are storing items in a living room, bedroom or kitchen.

- Vintage vanity cases, travel trunks and suitcases can regularly be found at flea markets and junk shops. Fill them with items you want out of the way, then stack them on the floor, on top of a wardrobe or even use them as a coffee table.

- Old bookcases, shelving units and chests of drawers can be given a new lease of life with a paintbrush or can of spray paint. This way you can match them perfectly to the rest of your room.

- Baskets hung on the wall create a versatile storage solution. Use them in the hallway for everyday clutter or hang them in the bedroom to hold your scarves, belts, jewellery and bags.

- Wooden or metal ex-factory trollies (wheeled carts) are great for storing items that may need to be moved around or be easily accessible. Craft supplies and kitchenware benefit from this type of storage.

Original shop fittings also make great storage solutions. Haberdashery (notions) cabinets, pigeon-hole shelving and multi-drawer filing units all look great in a home environment, and are usually large enough to store substantial amounts of family clutter.

Aside from furniture, you can add various containers around the home to store anything from magazines and books to toys and bed linen. The versatile wooden crate is a staple in any vintage home. You can paint and line them with fabric for a fresher look, or leave as is for a more rustic appearance. Old suitcases and trunks are useful for storing sheets, linens and towels in when not in use and are perfect for tidying away the children's toys once they've gone to bed. These can also be revamped by lining the inside with wallpaper, wrapping paper or even fabric.

For smaller items like buttons, jewellery, spare batteries or stationery supplies, keep an eye out for interesting vintage tins. There are lots to be found at markets and online, in an abundance of shapes, sizes, designs and colours. You may even find yourself amassing a small collection! Carved wooden boxes, china bowls and jugs, and vanity cases all feature regularly in charity (thrift) shops and at car boot (garage) sales, so watch out for a bargain that might just be the perfect size for your assortment of knitting needles or vintage silverware.

Top left *Dressers are not only for kitchens; they are perfect for craft supplies too. Collect jars, old tins and boxes to categorize your ribbons, buttons, threads and pins for a well-organized craft room.* **Top right** *These colourful baskets not only look fabulous but are handy for storing general clutter, such as keys and other everyday items, keeping your surfaces free of mess.* **Above left** *This clever idea is a good alternative to hooks in the hallway, and a simple, quick DIY project.* **Above right** *Vintage trollies (wheeled carts) are super-handy movable pieces in any room.*

shopkeepers at
home and at work

IN THIS SECTION WE TAKE A
CLOSER LOOK AT SOME OF THE
WORLD'S MOST UNIQUE AND
INTERESTING INDEPENDENT
SHOPS, AND PEEK INSIDE THE
HOMES OF THEIR OWNERS.

We learn a little bit about the creative
minds behind these spaces and discover
their style tips and decorating secrets.

We investigate the similarities and contrasts
between their shop and home aesthetics.
In some cases, the two spaces are almost
as one; in others the owner has made a
conscious choice to create differences in
their work and home environments. Both
approaches have resulted in interesting and
desirable locations, all of them inspirational.

Each section looks at different types of
venue – lifestyle boutiques, vintage vendors,
homeware stores, shops with cafes and,
finally, craft emporiums – each encompasses
distinct decor styles, from industrial and
vintage to Scandi and homespun.

Lifestyle Shops

Lifestyle shops offer a diverse range of goods aimed at enriching your home and everyday life. From soft furnishings and furniture to kitchenware, stationery or candles, such a wide range of design elements calls for a creative eye to compose coherent spaces that allow varied and often eclectic collections of items to sit comfortably together, while still preserving individual prominence. It is a styling method that translates well to the home.

Many lifestyle stores opt for simple walls and floors so as not to detract from their displays. Some choose to categorize their items by type or theme, while others create mixed arrangements. Despite their miscellaneous collections of merchandise, all the shop owners in this chapter clearly have their own distinct style, characterized by their personal curation of goods, their chosen methods of display and their decoration and styling preferences.

Often a simple, pristine, aesthetic using lots of white, accented with natural colours and materials, works well in an environment where there are a lot of interesting belongings to showcase.

DECORATING IDEAS TO TAKE HOME WITH YOU FROM LIFESTYLE STORES

1 Create atmosphere by zoning your living space into areas of interest divided by freestanding, open display units to showcase treasured possessions.

2 Keep walls and floors pared back so you can experiment with texture and colour on furniture. Let the objects do the talking.

3 Use repurposed furniture or renovate individual pieces yourself – use old crates or reclaimed wooden shelving to 'exhibit' your favourite items.

Opposite Atomic Garden, West Coast, USA

Atomic Garden

Reclaimed materials and vintage pieces are at the heart of the interior decor in this store where artisanal objects and sustainable items of kitchenalia work well on shelves of reclaimed wood. A subtle backdrop of neutral walls allows the quality of the objects to shine, with natural wood, metal and textiles giving a modern rustic aesthetic.

the shop

The establishment of lifestyle store Atomic Garden was a somewhat impulsive, but at the same time organic, career change for co-owners Adrienne Armstrong and Jamie Kidson. The two women were previously clothing designers, who met, not through work, but on the sidelines of a soccer field. While watching their children play, they developed a kinship – both were striving for a career with an emphasis on sustainability and craftsmanship, distancing themselves from the world of mass production. Originally they started looking into suitable companies to produce Adrienne's clothing line in this way. It didn't happen, but what came about instead was the discovery of many great makers and designers whose values matched theirs. The natural progression was to open a store selling the wares of these artisans

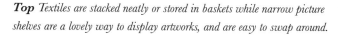

Top *Textiles are stacked neatly or stored in baskets while narrow picture shelves are a lovely way to display artworks, and are easy to swap around.*

Above *Almost anything looks good displayed inside a glass bottle.*

Right *This beautiful collection of kitchenware could easily translate to open shelving in the home. Group items of similar colours together for a coherent and eye-catching display.*

Opposite *Reclaimed wood, some repurposed from a local water tower, has been used for shelving, creating a natural and warm look.*

and promoting their shared ethos of well-designed, well-made products that have either a positive effect on the community or on the planet.

These ideals mean that everything they sell has some kind of story, and it was these stories that inspired the design of the store too. They chose to use materials that were natural and simplistic – lots of reclaimed wood, much of which was repurposed from a local building, and vintage pieces such as the large workshop bench, which is central to the store. With a wide and varied selection of goods, they didn't want the store to feel overwhelming, so pared-back display solutions were required, to complement the style of items they love. The two women spend a lot of time styling the store in a considered manner grouping together products that relate to each other in some way. Mini 'departments' are the result: for example, kitchenware, children's toys and clothes, soft furnishings and toiletries each have their own section, making browsing manageable while maintaining a natural flow.

Above The Atomic Garden ethos is one of good design and good craftsmanship. Most of their products are handmade by independent artisans and have a feeling of warmth and true character to them. **Opposite above** Items are grouped together in 'stories' or vignettes to make them feel homey. **Opposite below** A wire shelf with hooks makes good use of wall space and is used to display a collection of pennants and spools of ribbon.

the home

The shop owners agree that the store is constantly evolving. As new products arrive, the design dynamic changes, just as it does in a home when a new piece of furniture arrives. Striving to keep the space fresh and inspiring, they often incorporate different ideas into it – currently they are making a move towards celebrating California and its varying landscapes – mountains, desert, forest and the ocean. In fact, it is environmental diversity that Jamie loves about her Berkeley home. In one direction, she is five minutes from the base of a canyon hike, and two blocks in the other, she has the convenience of cafes, markets and shops. Jamie has lived in her current home for a little over a year, but has already carried out a substantial amount of restoration work.

Opposite *The kitchen has a functional yet classical authenticity, which is fitting for a home of this style. Jamie keeps clutter to a minimum and has introduced storage solutions such as wall-mounted knife holders and a traditional larder for easy accessibility.*

Below *Jamie's craftsman-style home was built by architect Walter Ratcliff in 1910. She has spent a long time restoring the property's original features to their former glory, while introducing retro furniture that blends well with the Arts and Crafts aesthetic.*

A wood-clad craftsman-style house, built in 1910 by a notable Berkeley architect, Walter Ratcliff, it has almost all of its original features, which Jamie has worked tirelessly to repair. She also tried to ensure that the newly installed kitchen and bathroom appeared as if they had always been there, choosing styles and colour palettes that blend seamlessly with the character of the building. A stickler for detail, she even aged some new brass window locks so they imitate what may have existed originally.

When it comes to decorating, Jamie explains, 'I would say my style has been evolving since I was little. I'm not sure I have a specific style, I decorate more in a response to the space and the way it feels.' She believes that daily life functions better in an

uncluttered environment and surrounds herself with a carefully chosen collection of objects that inspire her, or make her happy. While she sources things from flea markets, estate sales, eBay, Etsy and her own store, it is some of the more sentimental items that mean the most to her. Two clay unicorns made by one of her daughters, a cup crafted by her boyfriend, a potter, and a childhood toy tiger from 1966 make up a personal and meaningful edit of possessions. Another of her most treasured items, a jar of coloured sprinkles, dated 1942, was found

Above *Open shelving in the kitchen keeps things organized and within reach. Shelves above a window are good for utilizing dead space.*

Left *As a rule, Jamie keeps her interior quite minimal, yet still cosy. She says: "Keep it simple… we only need the essentials really – adding too much can end up taking away from the space. It is important to be mindful about what you bring into it.'*

at the estate sale of an artist. The rest of the family know how precious it is to her, and when someone knocked it over and cracked the glass, the culprit chose not to admit their blunder!

While Jamie has created an interior that is sympathetic to the original building, she is not afraid to mix in contemporary pieces that give the space a refreshing, updated aesthetic. Her background in design means she easily sees when something works in a space or not. As she says, 'It has to add to the space and not distract.' But her rule of thumb is, 'Surround yourself with things that make you happy. The energy that comes from that ethos will naturally make your space warm and inviting.' It is the authenticity that comes from decorating a home over time and keeping a sense of simplicity that has led to the creation of Jamie's classically beautiful home.

Above Jamie prefers an uncluttered environment with only useful or treasured items around her. She will never part with this little jar of sprinkles, which date from 1942. *Below* Dark paintings fit the decor perfectly. Jamie has owned the portrait of the woman for over 25 years.

ATOMIC GARDEN
5453 College Ave, Oakland, CA 94618, USA
www.atomicgardenoakland.com

Modern, bright and spacious is the overarching atmosphere inside lifestyle store Father Rabbit. Lots of white teamed with simplistic fixtures and fittings create clean lines and uncomplicated displays, highlighting a collection of household and lifestyle elements.

the shop

Father Rabbit is a modern-day general store stocking utilitarian yet carefully crafted products for everyday life. Owners Claudia Zinzan and Nick Hutchinson wanted to celebrate utility by presenting goods that have clear uses, are affordable but, above all, are of simple design.

Father Rabbit is a nickname that was given to Claudia by a dear friend of hers, and it has become an alter ego who oversees business operations – a witty description on their website describes him:

Above *Hang utensils from a metal bar painted white, using twine.*
Opposite *Father Rabbit's fresh and minimal interior allows the beautiful but utilitarian household items space to breathe.*

'Father Rabbit is not about grand gestures, but elevating those mundane everyday tasks. Embracing the simple pleasure of a well-made bed (with ironed pillowcases) and completing a clean bathroom with fresh cut flowers.' This fun use of a fictional character gets across the philosophy behind the brand, and both their Auckland stores and the couple's home clearly adhere to this appealing ethos of timelessness and purity.

In store, there is a strict colour palette of white, and despite their two retail spaces being quite different in architectural style – one is a modern building with polished concrete flooring and a large glass wall, the other a heritage-style setting – this blank canvas, coupled with their signature white shelving, tables and benches, sets the stage for the Father Rabbit aesthetic.

Their approach to styling the shops is to give their products lots of display space, and this technique also works well in the home. Objects are often grouped together in multiples and lined up neatly and evenly. The lighting is bright and clear, and there is minimal clutter, making the space feel refreshing and clean. The colour palette is muted, with lots of the items made from natural materials, creating a sense of calmness and integrity.

Clarity is important to the couple, so they have carefully curated the merchandise into mini departments that give plenty of visual ideas on how the many items could be stored and displayed at home. Wooden peg rails display brushes and kitchen tools, while buckets double up as storage items, and gardening tools are hung on a wall in vignettes, with pitchforks and spades suspended from wall hooks and pots, and brushes and birdhouses precisely laid out below.

This relaxed corner of Father Rabbit could be an actual fresh and bright bedroom space. It demonstrates how their goods could be used and displayed in a real home.

the home

Claudia and Nick's home incorporates a more relaxed level of precision and order than their shop, but it displays the same sense of minimalistic comfort. Colour is again mostly pared back, although there are some subtle additions, such as the pastel cushions on the sofa, and the pea green walls in the hallway. Claudia used to be a colour consultant for Aalto Colour, a New Zealand paint brand, so the green hallway shade is a custom colour mixed specifically for her, descriptively named 'Zinzan Hall'.

The house is testament to the fact that you can make a beautiful home on a budget. When they bought the place, they weren't in a position financially to carry out expensive renovations, so used their initiative and thought creatively about how to improve the space. The living and dining space was a basic 1960s lean-to, so rather than rebuild a modern extension, they clad the interior walls and painted them white, which they felt was more characteristic of the original building.

Nick used his DIY skills to make some furniture, such as the kitchen island and the under-sink cupboard in the bathroom. Claudia was in charge of sourcing accessories and as well as using some of their own product range, they sourced items from salvage yards and internet auction sites.

FATHER RABBIT
20 Normanby Road, Mount Eden, Auckland, New Zealand
www.fatherrabbit.com

Above The couple were thrifty when it came to their kitchen refit. They made the island themselves, adding a stainless-steel top, with shelving made from MDF. *Opposite left* Claudia and Nick like to mix architectural salvage yard finds with contemporary designs, which come together in this corner of their living space. *Opposite right* A tongue-and-groove wall and open shelving, holding white china and glassware are fresh and timeless.

Oh Hello Friend

This eclectic, inspiring store oozes creativity, thanks to owner and well-known blogger Danni. Clever ideas for display and decor can be spotted everywhere, with plants and flowers being a significant element in the creation of this inviting space.

YOU ARE
EXACTLY
WHERE
YOU NEED
TO BE

the shop

Oh Hello Friend started out as Danni Hong's successful design and lifestyle blog. The name originates from an affectionate greeting Danni and her best friend used to give to each other in high school. After five years of blogging and establishing her brand, Danni decided it was time to open her own retail space, inspired by her parents, who both ran stores when she was growing up. She set up shop in Fullerton, California, in 2013.

As a blogger, Danni is well versed in internet research and spends a lot of time searching for new products online, as well as attending trade fairs. Her stock is a mix of homeware, stationery, party supplies and gifts, and her eye for design means the merchandise is styled and displayed beautifully. The space has a clean, bright feel, and while the majority of her products are new, Danni has incorporated her love of vintage by using old tables, chairs and suitcases as display units. She has also added wooden crates in various ways – some to simply hold products, some to add height to a display, and in one area she has fixed a group of crates to the wall as shelving, adding small air plants and other items inside. She says that while she did a little research into store design, generally she took inspiration from how she has decorated her own home, when deciding how to create the look at the shop.

The cash register area is a feature of the store, with large lightbulb lettering spelling out the initials of the shop's name, set against a wall papered in pages from an old dictionary. The counter is made from reclaimed wood, and social-media-savvy Danni has added a decal of their hashtag, which customers can then use to tag pictures and posts online. Suspended from the ceiling above the cash register area is an old wooden ladder, which has been draped in greenery. The same structure would also make a great feature in a kitchen if used to display a *batterie de cuisine*. Fresh flowers and indoor plants have been used throughout the store to create a homey atmosphere while also demonstrating how some of her products can be used to display them.

It's clear that Danni has an eye for detail. In the area where she holds creative workshops, the tables are dressed to perfection, a mini cake table displays colourful macaroons, vintage plates and stripy straws. Even the selection of pens left out for participants are pretty. A freestanding screen separates the workshop space from the main shop and is covered in book pages, echoing the feature wall near the cash register.

Top *The workshop area is decorated with handmade items and wire-framed artefacts – a beautiful space for creativity and socializing.*

Bottom *Some of the great decorating ideas here include carnival lighting, pages from old books used as wallpaper and a plant-draped ladder suspended from the ceiling as a point of visual interest.*

Opposite *A quote stencilled on the floor creates impact and brings a touch of humour to the store.*

Danni often uses colour to tie her displays together. Here, a minty green shade mixes with white and cream on a pretty table of wares. She creates height using old crates or boxes on tables, as well as standing tall pieces of freestanding furniture with open shelving as space markers. She then adds flowers and small plants throughout the store, bringing a touch of nature, a sense of hominess and a certain authenticity to the space.

Danni's mix of homeware, stationery, party supplies and gifts are beautifully enhanced and easy to view when placed in vintage glass-fronted cabinets. The space has neutral walls and plain wooden floors so that the interesting pieces of freestanding furniture become eye-catching features in their own right while doubling up as highly practical storage and display units.

the home

Surrounded by lovely things all day, Danni says she tries not to bring too much home from the shop, and tends to keep her personal space separate in terms of interior style. While there are similarities – white walls, wooden floors, lots of colour and quirky objects – the emphasis at home is on her carefully curated collection of vintage finds. The house itself needed lots of work initially – Danni replaced the kitchen and bathrooms, installed some new flooring and re-stained some of the original floors, as well as painting the entire interior. They also had the kitchen floor skimmed in polished concrete, which Danni loves and says is super-easy to keep clean.

The couple regularly visit antique markets, auctions and thrift shops to search out interesting items for their home. One such object is the battery-powered bright yellow scooter, which resides in their living

Above Danni fills her home with items she's sourced from flea markets and thrift shops, but keeps the look up to date by adding bright, bold patterns via soft furnishings.

Opposite The yellow, battery-powered scooter is a favourite flea market find. It's both a source of conversation and a focal point, like the eclectic mix of prints on the wall.

home
sweet
home

Left *Industrial shelving houses vintage treasures; while geometric bedding and a floral rug bring a contemporary, feminine feel to the bedroom.*

Below *The sunny colour palette is a running theme throughout the house, with vintage touches like embroidered sunflowers.*

Opposite *Danni's stationery and postage ephemera dominate her workspace.*

room. Being a big fan of yellow, Danni was naturally drawn to it. The piece adds an element of surprise to the living space, and it ties in seamlessly with the sunny colour scheme.

While Danni's home is full of interesting vintage finds, she has kept the look up to date with fresh white walls and the addition of modern geometric prints via cushions, rugs and bedspreads. It's clear she has paid lots of attention to the styling of every room, while the space still maintains a lived-in, homey feel. She has created vignettes that mix intriguing objects, art, flowers and personal items such as photos, signifying elements of the couple's

lives. The grouping of vintage globes represents their love of travel, while Danni's enviable collection of stationery and postage ephemera is a by-product of her graphic design background.

Personality truly shines through in both Danni's home and store, resulting in friendly and inviting spaces. Her advice for achieving this? Only buy what you love and stay true to who you are.

OH HELLO FRIEND
122 N. Harbour Blvd., Fullerton, CA 92832, USA
www.ohhellofriend.com

Summer Camp

This shop in Ojai, California, is a perfect example of how to repurpose a building. The mix of mid-century design and handmade artisan products makes for an interesting browse, while gathering plenty of decorating ideas inspired by the great outdoors.

the shop

When Rachel and Mike Graves spotted a 'for lease' sign outside an old gas station in Ojai, California, they knew it was the perfect location for the shop that they'd dreamed of having for years. The mid-century architecture and the light-filled space fitted their dream in every respect.

The Summer Camp name is a cute, nostalgic nod to Rachel's childhood days as a girl scout, while capturing the outdoors feel they've created inside the shop. An abundance of potted plants, a full-size canoe and chunky logs used as display tables all help to achieve this look. Much of their product range also offers the dream of the perfect camping weekend – vintage flasks, cosy blankets, gas lamps and binoculars are all stylishly displayed and would encourage even the most reluctant camper to pack up their tent and don their walking boots.

The couple love to support small businesses and craftspeople, and say much of the store's furniture is made locally, while the plant life comes from a nearby farm. They carry lots of products by local Ojai makers, as well as others from across the US and are meticulous in selecting a cohesive collection of new and vintage items.

Styling is one of the most important aspects of their store. 'We want the shop to feel familiar and cosy, like you have been there before and don't want to leave.' They regularly update their displays and move things around, to keep the space looking fresh.

Above A mid-century converted petrol (gas) station houses Summer Camp in Ojai, California. Here, a salmon pink picnic area welcomes customers and hints at the outdoors theme of the merchandise.

Opposite An old ladder has been cleverly converted into a display unit, while plants and chopped logs continue the 'back-to-nature' aesthetic that works well in most homes.

the home

The 'Summer Camp' home is a small redwood cabin-style bungalow in Ventura, California. Despite the small proportions of the house – it is only about 46.5 square metres (500 square feet) – they fell in love with its charm and the beautiful outside space it had to offer. The interior wood panelling gives the cabin a warm and cosy feeling, but numerous windows mean it doesn't feel dark or enclosed. In such a small space, possessions need to be edited and chosen carefully, and the couple have decorated with lots of plants and a few favourite items. Even the kitchen is simple and uncluttered. Open shelving displays a

Top A small kitchen calls for minimal clutter, so a simple display of glassware, cups and plates is all that is needed.

Opposite The compact cabin-style home is cosy and inviting, while the mid-century furniture adds a layer of retro chic.

simple set of plates, mugs and glassware with a few pops of copper, while a vintage food mixer adds a subtle dash of colour.

In the living room, bohemian chic mixes with mid-century design. A vintage Danish desk, bar cart and slat-bench coffee table combine with kilim pillows and a vintage Turkish rug for a simplistic but effortlessly cool aesthetic. In the bedroom, traditional textiles such as a striped blanket by time-honoured American brand Pendelton work perfectly next to the clean design of mid-century pieces.

Running Summer Camp has definitely influenced how Rachel and Mike approach their home decor. It has given them a more critical eye for selecting objects and how to put them together. They often

frequent flea markets and thrift shops to discover talented makers – it means that their home inevitably ends up with some of their best finds, showcasing mid century with a rustic twist.

SUMMER CAMP
1020 West Ojai Avenue, Ojai, CA 93023, USA
www.shopsummercamp.com

Above *As their home is small, Rachel and Mike love that they have an outdoor area – it is the perfect spot in which to stretch out and enjoy a warm, Californian evening.*

Opposite top *In the bedroom, traditional fabrics combine effortlessly with the clean lines of a classic Eames rocker.*

Opposite bottom *Knitted cushions are piled up on a vintage sofa – a classic juxtaposition of old and new that is a popular styling trick in many lifestyle stores.*

The Hambledon

Since it opened in 1999, The Hambledon has aimed to be a kind of department store but just selling the 'good stuff'. Homewares and lifestyle pieces and their associated friends live on the ground floor of the building.

the shop

Victoria Suffield, owner of The Hambledon in Winchester, UK, says 'I've always wanted the shop to reflect a whole life.' She sells things she loves: clothes, decorative items and books among them.

Visual merchandising is hugely important to Victoria and her team. The beauty of the building has been allowed to shine through, and the interior is kept simple, with white walls and highlights in a specific paint colour called Hambledon Grey. The floors have been stripped back to the bare wood, and classic Philippe Starck Romeo lights are unobtrusive and tasteful. Simple built-in shelving houses products in an orderly fashion, while select pieces of vintage furniture act as the perfect calm and cohesive setting for anything from books and independent magazines to haberdashery notions and party supplies.

__Above and opposite__ An uncomplicated approach to styling, combined with bare textured floors and furniture, creates great warmth.

PIE SET

FALCON
FALCON
FALCON
FALCON

PLATE SET

the home

Victoria's 1930s family home is situated just
ten-minutes away from the store, and was quite
dilapidated when purchased. But the original features
and space drew them in, and it soon became a
beautiful home, thanks to Victoria's simple styling.
A plain backdrop of white and grey highlights her
collection of paintings, objects, classic pieces of
furniture and vintage finds.

Uncluttered decor allows the architectural
detailing of the building to shine – the parquet
flooring, fireplace, windows and doors are features in
themselves. Victoria has simply highlighted them by
adding favourite pieces of art, a restrained amount
of furniture and pops of colour via textiles such as
the wonderful woven rug in the sitting room.

Being surrounded by 'things' all day at work,
Victoria prefers simplicity at home.

Opposite *Mid-century chairs are a stylish fit for the 1930s interior, while the colourful woven rug is a strong focal point in the room.*

Right *An iconic chair designed by Norman Cherner sits proudly under a gallery wall of mixed-size artwork, creating interesting shapes and lines. A single hydrangea stem softens the scene.*

Bottom *Victoria is not a big shopper when it comes to things for her own home, but she enjoys displaying some of her most treasured items. These shelves look like they could tell a thousand stories.*

Previous spread *Two pieces of shop display that Victoria can never part with are the marble-topped counter and the large vintage letters that spell out 'Atelier'. She says these are permanent fixtures, as she has become quite sentimental about them.*

THE HAMBLEDON
10 The Square, Winchester, Hampshire SO23 9ES, UK
www.thehambledon.com

the shop

Stepping inside Caravan is almost like stepping into an impeccably styled front room rather than a retail space. Bursting with unique finds, where generally only one or two of each item is on display, it gives the carefully selected range of homewares room to breathe. It may even make you feel that if you buy these objects, your home might just become as effortlessly cool as this shop based in London's East End. The store's look is a perfect reflection of its owner, Emily Chalmers, a stylist and author, whose own unique style balances femininity with eccentricity, and mixes old and new with ease. All the items for sale are either beautiful, quirky or fun; most are all three traits rolled into one. You are sure to find something in store that you never knew you needed but can't live without – a wall-mounted donkey's head perhaps?!

Not only is Caravan's aesthetic influenced by Emily's personal style and her work as an interiors stylist, it is also dictated by the architecture of the building. The shop has moved numerous times over the years, this being its fourth home, and the way Emily has displayed her items has changed according to the space itself. Currently, it is a late 1960s building, with clean lines and a simplistic feel, so Emily has opted to keep the shop less crowded but added a set of reclaimed doors for visual interest.

Top *Wall decoration comprises china plates, a swan's head, a handbag and a badger-shaped rug all confined in one small area.*

Bottom *Emily considered various options to separate her shop floor from her admin area – fabric, screens, sliding doors – but found an old set of doors on a reclamation yard's website and knew they were perfect.*

Opposite *A quirky and humorous mix of beautiful vintage pieces and contemporary designs.*

Overleaf *Vintage one-offs and high-street finds are an inspiration.*

Caravan

Eccentric but stylish is a good description of East London boutique Caravan. It highlights elements of the building while mixing vintage and whimsical modern-day designs.

the home

A similar approach has been taken with Emily's residential space. She formerly lived in a large warehouse conversion, which was completely open-plan with high ceilings. It needed large pieces of furniture to fill it, and Emily partitioned off areas with drapes of fabric. But today, she and her family live in an ex-local authority building from the 1960s, which she affectionately calls a 'box'. A far cry from her previous residence, Emily says she initially worried about living with low ceilings, but in fact she adores the house and says it is well planned architecturally and surprisingly light and airy.

Aside from knocking through the kitchen wall, removing a stair banister and pulling up the laminate flooring, they have not done much to the property structurally. Emily created a plain backdrop using her favourite off-white paint colour – the same colour used in the shop – and the floor was given a budget makeover with a basic levelling compound that was sanded and varnished – a good solution for creating a blank canvas for furniture. Emily then unleashed her creativity on the space. It is only the wall in the living area that steps away from the muted setting –

the exposed brick was in fact a happy accident but they have grown to love the tactile quality it adds to the room and the unexpected nature of such a feature in a building of this period.

The natural shades of the brickwork blend well with the furnishings in the room. Emily's favourite blue floral swivel chair (pages 104–5), a cheap thrift shop find reupholstered in vintage fabric, adds a feminine, contrasting touch to the raw wall, while a shiny gold beanbag allows a hint of glamour to creep in. Elsewhere in her home, Emily has many items that combine design, integrity and personality.

Above left, centre and right Emily incorporates lots of favourite items from her shop at home. The flower-shaped rug in the kitchen is such a piece. The large swan planters and decorative animals have many uses indoors and out. Emily even uses one for storing her daughter's toys.

Opposite A polished concrete floor might initially seem more suited to an industrial interior, but here it is a stylish juxtaposition against the more feminine, glamorous elements in the room.

CARAVAN
5 Ravenscroft Street, London E2 7SH, UK
www.caravanstyle.com

Vintage Shops

Many of today's purveyors of vintage goods have changed the perception of dusty, poky antique shops, crammed to the rafters with random and unloved bric-a-brac. Personally, I enjoy a good rummage in these types of shop to unearth forgotten finds that can be brought back to life, but many folk find it difficult to see past the clutter and simply consider it to be junk. However a visit to any one of these vintage shops would uncover beautifully curated collections of vintage wares that have been cared for, styled and displayed to make you fall for the nostalgic charm of items from the past. They also show how vintage furniture and decorative pieces can be brought up to date for a 21st-century home – edgy not aged.

DUSTY DECO (page 112) utilizes a warehouse-style space to showcase its mid-century furniture, extravagant lighting and flamboyant seating. At HOME BARN (page 126) individual 'rooms' have been created within a vast agricultural space and at KABINETT AND KAMMER (page 142) a cornucopia of painted furniture and striking vignettes cannot fail to provide inspiration.

DECORATING IDEAS TO TAKE HOME WITH YOU FROM VINTAGE STORES

1 Take time out to enjoy browsing for unique finds in vintage or antique stores to source the perfect finishing touch, whether it's a vase or a painted table.

2 It's fine to mix eras when decorating with vintage furniture. Create cohesion by means of a colour palette or by grouping similar objects together.

3 Curate your own collection of favourite finds – anything from apothecary jars or vintage advertising posters to kitchenalia or wooden tools.

Opposite Kabinett & Kammer, USA

Dusty Deco

An industrial warehouse area is the setting for the Dusty Deco store. This striking open-plan space accommodates a wide range of vintage furniture, all carefully styled in inspirational room sets that mix textures and materials, each room complemented by unique lighting and stunning photographic art.

the shop

Husband and wife team Edin and Lina Kjellvertz have Dusty Springfield and a bottle of wine to thank for their fabulous Stockholm-based store. It was during a trip to Barcelona, sipping wine and listening to Springfield tunes that the pair decided they would set up shop. Frequent travellers, they found they were constantly buying things for their home but their apartment was filling up fast, so it became clear that a shop meant they could continue with their buying trips and just sell their finds instead.

Above left Each piece here appears to reflect and complement the statement light fitting – allowing it to be the focal point – while the colour palette and materials seem cohesive. *Above right* Neon 'text' lighting is bang on trend at the moment. Dusty Deco's pink version really pops against the dark walls behind their counter. *Opposite* The warehouse 'living spaces' demonstrate how furniture could look in a home setting.

They cite travelling as a major influence on the style of both their store and home; from restaurants and hotels to shops and the outdoors, they are always gathering ideas. They wanted the retail space to be almost an extension of their home, so the two locations have clear similarities in style. The look is eclectic, but with a strong preference for vintage. Edin says they have always loved vintage: 'The quality is so much better than newly made pieces, every item tells a story and it is better for the environment to reuse than to throw things away.' But it is within the vintage genre that the eclectic mix is created – from American industrial to slick Italian brass and velvet – the couple are drawn to many different pieces of furniture, decorative items and

Above *This hot pink leather sofa is a bold choice, but with pared-back textiles and white walls, Edin and Lina prove it can work.*

Previous page *Dusty Deco stocks a varied mix of vintage styles – American industrial next to mid-century design and shiny brass from Italy. Their clever styling shows how well the different looks can merge.*

artwork, and they buy what they love rather than sticking to an era or style.

For them, the styling of their store is the most important part and they make changes on a fortnightly basis, and more frequently when large items are sold. They want all the senses to be tantalized during a visit to the shop, so spend a lot of time on how it looks, the way it smells and the music they play. It's a large warehouse space, so they try to create smaller areas for a sense of home, using a mixture of materials such as wood, metal and textiles, then adding lighting schemes and artwork.

The warehouse venue seems the perfect spot for their wares. Their industrial pieces such as the large factory lights above the cash register sit easily in this setting, while slick glass and metal pieces juxtapose against the rough textures of the walls and floor. They have recently been focusing on photo art, which brings an added contemporary edge – something they clearly enjoy in their own home too.

Top *A colourful agglomeration of freestanding vintage globe lights would create a focal point in any style of room.*

Left *Cactuses are a relatively easy houseplant to opt for if your're green-fingered, plus their structured form works particularly well in a mid-century-style space.*

the home

Edin and Lina live in an old building in the south of Stockholm. Built in 1888, the apartment has original wooden floors and the ceilings are nearly 4m (13ft) high – they instantly fell in love with them. Despite not living here long, the couple have already created a super-stylish space, filling it with their favourite vintage possessions.

Their home is a living example of how to furnish a space with Dusty Deco merchandise. They've mixed rustic wood, industrial pieces, shiny metallics, splashes of colour and striking photography. Despite admitting he is slightly tired of the term 'eclectic', Edin says that this is probably the best way to describe their style. Creating an interesting look comes from being brave, daring to mix the unexpected, daring to be different.

DUSTY DECO
Hornstullstrand 7, Stockholm, Sweden
www.dustydeco.tictail.com

Above An extensive collection of photography books is stacked on surfaces to give height to a display, but are also easy to access. **Opposite above** *The gold candlesticks and lamp base tie in well with discreet gold handles on custom-built units, creating a subtle touch of luxury. Contemporary artwork is a chic addition that adds another layer of decoration.* **Opposite below** *Rustic wood, floral patterns and shiny metallics all work harmoniously in the Stockholm apartment.*

Beam & Anchor

Exposed brickwork, wooden beams and a concrete floor complement vintage wares and stylish Scandinavian design at Beam & Anchor. The eclectic space offers tips for combining different looks, plus ideas for walls and floors.

the shop

Sometimes in life, when things don't feel quite right, it is necessary to take a step back and re-evaluate what is important to you and what makes you happy, and this is exactly what Robert and Jocelyn Rahn did before opening Beam & Anchor in 2012. The couple felt static in their careers – Robert as a therapist and Jocelyn working in the education sector. They started to imagine what their lives would be like if they were working together in a creative business, something completely different from their current jobs. During a sabbatical from work, Robert wrote a business plan, and from there they got the ball rolling; soon after, Beam & Anchor was born.

Despite their previous careers, the couple were not without experience in their new field. Robert had taken up furniture-making years before and Jocelyn has two art-based degrees, so they found that opening a shop selling vintage furniture and design products came naturally to them. The space they chose to house their goods is a gritty industrial warehouse with concrete floors, bare brickwork and wooden beams. They've kept this stripped-back interior, adding factory-style lighting and wall panelling made from reclaimed wood, creating warmth.

Opposite *Industrial furniture in metal and wood hold Beam & Anchor's mix of vintage and Scandinavian wares.*

Below *A large warehouse space is the perfect opportunity to go big, so Robert and Jocelyn hung a canoe from the ceiling for a striking statement.*

To add colour and interest to the large expanse of concrete floor, they commissioned a woman from the Klamath people – a Native American tribe that inhabit southern Oregon – to design and paint some traditional imagery for them. They've made a feature of the paying area, repurposing an old bar, complete with foot rail and padded velvet. This was salvaged from an old hotel that had burned down in the San Juan islands, off Seattle. Above hangs a custom-made light box stating the store's name.

The aesthetic of their inventory is a harmonious mix of old and new – large pieces of old wooden and metal furniture, which have a rawness to them, alongside contemporary Scandinavian design products, which are fresh and sleek. This is a place in which to feel relaxed and inspired, as well as shop.

Above *Textiles are imaginatively displayed from wooden dowels fixed to the wall, while cushions nestle in an industrial trolley (cart).*
Opposite above *An old bar, salvaged from a hotel has been repurposed into Beam & Anchor's cash desk, and a custom-made lightbox bears their logo – a fun idea.* **Opposite below** *Traditional Native American imagery is painted onto the concrete, a great solution for adding colour and interest to a stripped-back floor, which could easily be re-created with a stencil and some floor or spray paint.*

the home

As for their own home life, the couple moved house and had twins at the end of 2014, but luckily for them they have a 'home away from home' above their store while they prepare their new house for family life. The space is a fine example of how to decorate using items from their shop. The interior structure is of course very similar – plenty of space, lots of brick, old wood and a fabulous industrial green metal door.

They've created some shelving from old scaffold boards which also acts as a feature wall, making a backdrop for a comfy seating area. Worn leather chairs mix with a more contemporary-style sofa, and a selection of Navajo cushions add comfort, colour and texture. A trio of modern vases sits atop the repurposed coffee table, contrasting well with the surrounding rustic wood.

Robert and Jocelyn say that when their new home is complete, it will be very reminiscent of the look they've created here and in the shop, as this is very much their signature style.

BEAM & ANCHOR
2710 N. Interstate Ave, Portland, OR 97227, USA
www.beamandanchor.com

Above *Planks of reclaimed wood have been used in a unique way here, creating a layered, three-dimensional wall covering.*

Above left *A unique collection of vintage paintings are ranged around a metal industrial storage cabinet to create a homey feel.*

Home Barn

In the countryside just outside London, this cavernous old barn is filled with a hand-picked collection of vintage goods. The space feels homey, despite its vast size, as all the furniture is impeccably styled and displayed. A photo-worthy scene can be spotted in every direction you choose to look in.

the shop

Nestled in the pretty village of Little Marlow in the Buckinghamshire countryside is Home Barn. With its modest, wood-panelled entrance, the 17th-century tithe barn seems unassuming, but step inside and the most spectacular of timber interiors greets you, which may just take your breath away with its rustic charm and the treasures that await your perusal. A listed building, the structure is pretty much exactly as it would have been when used for its original agricultural purpose but now, instead of hay bales and farming machinery, every corner is filled with an abundance of vintage delights.

The ramshackle barn was acquired back in 2010 by sisters-in-law Sally and Sarah Wilkie and their husbands. All sharing a passion for

Left *Sally and Sarah hope that people will feel at home when browsing the barn, and they have created a children's section where everything is of course for sale, but kids can also play while their parents shop.*

Opposite *The vast barn that houses Home Barn is an impressive structure. A wide, open interior like this demands similarly impressive lighting, such as this grand chandelier – not to mention huge curtains and mammoth rugs.*

interiors and a love of vintage objects and antiques, having a shop was their dream, and the old barn was the perfect backdrop for a unique shopping experience. It took them two months to clear the space of dead Christmas trees, pumpkins and other agricultural items, and without wanting to interfere with the rustic feel of the building, they simply added some power points and light fittings to transform it into a working retail space.

The interior is huge and open-plan, but Sally and Sarah have managed to design areas within the barn that feel like individual rooms. This has created a more defined and homey feel, making it more manageable for browsing. From a desk with task lighting and plan chests forming an office area to a kitchen space displaying dressers and cupboards accessorized with vintage kitchenalia, their styling demonstrates decorating ideas that can be translated to their customers' own homes. A colourful corner filled with vintage toys and children's books is also perfect for the kids to play in while parents browse the rest of the barn, making everyone feel at home.

Along with the rest of their creative team, the pair often restyle the barn to keep it fresh and appealing.

At Home Barn, Sally and Sarah have styled small segments to represent an area or room of the home. This 'workspace' is complete with vintage filing drawers, a typewriter and a wonderful old desk chair.

Sarah's own home workspace is peppered with interesting objects. A collection of vintage bead cards are displayed on the wall using bulldog clips, while a set of chemistry bottles holds floral cuttings and a Royal Mail postbox stands off to the right.

the home

Sarah and Mark moved to their 100-year-old cottage ten years ago, after craving a more relaxed pace of family life away from their previous Central London lifestyles.

The cottage was initially dark and small, with deep aubergine walls downstairs and canary yellow upstairs, but the couple have transformed it into a light-filled and spacious family home. They added a large extension with big windows and roof lights, creating a pale backdrop against which their vintage furniture and treasures could shine.

With many of their possessions reflecting the Home Barn vintage aesthetic, the couple admit that they meet in the middle when it comes to styling their home – Mark's background in graphics is evident in various pieces of typographic art around the place, while the couple mix the rustic, aged look with cleaner lines confidently and also incorporate unique finds from their travels, such as some lovely blue metallic bottles they picked up while on holiday in France. These still contain lead shot for the hunting of wild boar. Family life is also incorporated into their interiors, as the children's artwork created using

Above A perfect sideboard vignette requires objects of varying sizes, shapes and forms. Stacks of books are a great way to add height to smaller items, and glass cloches protect precious pieces. The backdrop of the mirrored window frame is a great addition here.

Opposite Sarah's living room is a warm and inviting space, centred around the wood-burning stove. The colour coordinated spines of her book collection are an eye-catching feature.

vintage letterpress, old stencils and lino-cuts are on display in several rooms.

Sarah has interesting items both large and small in their home – from an old Royal Mail postbox in the office and a huge mirrored window frame in the sitting room to tiny glass bottles on the coffee table and intriguing ephemera displayed on shelves. Even the bathroom has not been overlooked, with lotions and potions stored in vintage pharmaceutical bottles, and a trio of framed illustrated prints, complementing the beautiful freestanding bath.

As with their store, no corner has been neglected in the style stakes. Sarah ensures each and every room delights the eyes with its vintage charm, demonstrating perfectly how the Home Barn aesthetic translates to a modern family home.

Above left *This shelving unit in the office works hard. As well as being storage for paperwork, it also displays an intriguing collection of vintage ephemera – from old bingo cards to unusual measuring tools.*

Above right *Old pharmacy bottles can be repurposed as containers for bathroom essentials, meaning no more ugly plastic bottles on display.*

Opposite *The house was originally dark and small, but a modern extension transformed it into a fresh, light-filled space – a perfect blank canvas for their rustic furniture and vintage finds.*

HOME BARN
Marlow Road, Little Marlow, Bourne End,
Buckinghamshire SL7 3RR, UK
www.homebarnshop.co.uk

Vintage Factory

Pastel colours, pretty florals and a dollop of nostalgia are all found inside Swedish store Vintage Factory. The 1950s greatly influence this shop's look, yet it is kept up to date with contemporary illustration, design and decoration.

the shop

'Like a kid in a candy shop' is how Linda Hansson and her co-owners Emma Sundh and Louise Lemming want their customers to feel when they enter Vintage Factory. Filled with a delectable collection of vintage clothes, homewares, books and accessories, the trio even went as far as to take inspiration from nostalgic candy stores of yesteryear. They painted a harlequin pattern on the wooden floor and used lots of sweet pastel shades for a retro fifties vibe.

The store came about after the three released a book together about vintage parties. They wanted to continue their collaboration and started to look for a shared office space. They started discussing projects that could make use of the two available rooms. Soon, their shared dream of running a store filled with beautiful things came to fruition, and they immediately got to work, opening the doors in 2013.

With a background in visual merchandising and journalism, Linda has real flair for styling the store and regularly updates their window displays to keep things interesting for their customers as well as themselves. While a large proportion of their stock is vintage, they also sell a carefully selected range of contemporary items, such as stationery by Rifle Paper Co, prints by Swedish illustrators and some organic clothing for children. This mixture of fresh 'modern vintage' and contemporary items together in one place is unique in Stockholm.

Above left *The Vintage Factory owners buy what they love for their shop. From vintage china to contemporary illustrations to floral tea dresses, all their goods blend beautifully for a feminine vintage vibe.*

Opposite *There are cute ideas galore in this corner of the shop: rolls of pretty wrapping paper fill a vintage cookie tin, and paper pompoms hanging from the ceiling add texture and depth.*

the home

Linda's love of vintage is a way of life, and she admits that when she visits flea markets, the eternal question is, 'Shall I take it home or to the shop?' Luckily for her, if it does go to the shop, the perk of the job is she can change her mind later and bring it home. Unsurprisingly, Linda's home also has its roots in the past. The apartment is housed in a beautiful brick building, built in 1927, and has original oak parquet flooring throughout. Linda approaches the styling of her home differently from the shop interior. While her core style is evidently similar, in store she is more inventive, aiming to inspire and boost creativity, while at home she strives to create a comfortable, relaxed and livable space for herself and her family.

Her sitting room is the epitome of this laid-back, lived-in philosophy. A soft colour palette makes for a calming ambience, mismatched cushions and vases of pretty flowers add a cosy touch, while the collection of books and musical equipment suggest that the room is very much a family space in use.

Linda loves how a simple pot of paint and a brush can completely transform a room in a matter of hours and that is exactly what she has done in her bedroom recently. The dark blue shade she has chosen is a bold choice – but one that has paid off, as the room – despite blue generally being considered a cool colour – has warmth and richness to it. Painting the door, ceiling and a small section above the picture rail white has kept a lightness to the space, while the red vintage chair and the use of textiles such as velvet and Liberty prints have added a touch of luxury. The uncluttered simplicity she has achieved makes for an inviting spot to relax, read or sleep.

VINTAGE FACTORY
Svandammsvägen 8, Stockholm, Sweden
www.vintagefabriken.se

This page *Feminine vintage style is subtle and relaxed and definitely not twee in Linda's sitting room. The rich plum shade of the armchair combines with the softer pastel colours beautifully and the chunky old suitcases seem to bring a touch of masculinity to the space.*

Opposite left *Linda has accompanied the beautiful white piano with an embroidered vintage stool and has topped it with her favourite vases, candles and an old typewriter.*

Opposite right *A rich warming blue on the walls in the bedroom is welcoming and cosy.*

Empire Vintage

Long-standing Melbourne store Empire Vintage has a darker, more atmospheric and slightly dramatic take on the vintage look. An intriguing exterior leads to an inviting interior, where industrial style meets a utilitarian aesthetic, with a hint of glamour and theatricality thrown in for good measure.

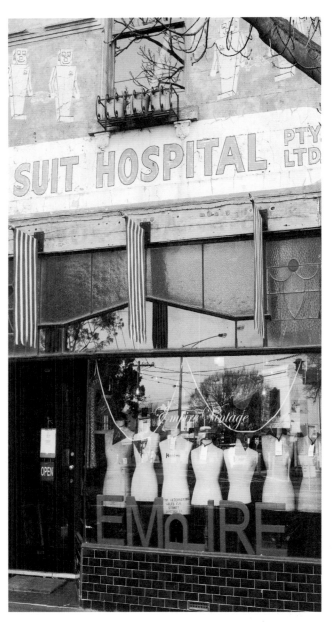

the shop

Empire Vintage has been a fixture of the Albert Park area of Melbourne since 1994. This well-established shop is owned by Lynda Gardener, an interiors stylist, who also works with her business partner Amanda, decorating and styling bars, restaurants, cafes and private homes. Lynda originally opened the store on a whim. After driving past the shop unit one day, she thought how nice it would be to have her own retail space where she could sell some of her collection of vintage finds. At the time, the way she styled and displayed her wares was quite unique to the vintage market, so she stood out from the typical dusty old antique shops and encouraged a new type of buyer. Despite being based in a quiet area, Empire Vintage has thrived as word of mouth helped to build her customer base over the years.

Left *Empire Vintage has a truly intriguing shop frontage. The Victorian building was originally a 'suit hospital' for invisible mending and repairs to suits. Lynda loves that the building's history is still visible and would never paint over it while it is under her watch.*

Opposite above *Much of Lynda's stock — white ceramics, linens, glassware and enamelware — is neutral in colour and highlighted by a dark, moody paint colour on the interior walls.*

The store has seen many different guises in its 20-year history. Originally Lynda's aesthetic was rustic country, with a focus on painted furniture, before going through a more feminine stage of florals, chandeliers and white furniture. She generally gives the space an entire makeover every five years, and the latest one has been the most extensive. She installed pigeonholes and floor-to-ceiling shelving to create the look of an old hardware store and painted the walls dark for a more moody, atmospheric vibe. Her stock has an industrial edge, with an overall colour palette of neutral whites, greys and the occasional splash of red.

Right Lynda has taken inspiration from traditional hardware stores by using a wall of pigeonhole shelving and glass cabinets to display her delightfully varied vintage stock.

the home

Lynda says the store is a direct reflection of the style she has in her own home at any given time. When sourcing, she always buys for her home first and then the shop. Her current residential space – an inner city warehouse – was originally a mattress factory. When she acquired it, over 15 years ago, it was totally dilapidated and unlivable. The entire ground floor had no windows, there was asbestos in all of the ceilings, and the floors were blue and the walls brown, but somehow Lynda spotted the potential. She has transformed the place, turning a garage into a lounge room, and a toilet block into a beautiful bedroom. She also added a central courtyard to bring light into the lower area, and created a roof garden to enjoy the sunshine.

Inside, the open-plan living space is light and bright, a contrast to the darker palette at Empire Vintage, but her choice of furniture and accessories is comparable. Again, a natural colour palette of white, cream and brown is dominant with a few dashes of brighter colour such as blue or yellow. Furniture is mainly industrial mixed with some French country-style items. She has accessorized with lots of old books, paintings and taxidermy, creating interesting and beautiful vignettes in every corner.

The sitting area has a more French feel, with faded calico and striped linens and a collection of oil paintings on the wall, while in the dining room there is a wall display of male portraits collected from all over the world.

EMPIRE VINTAGE
63 Cardigan Place, Albert Park, Victoria 3206, Australia
www.empirevintage.com.au

Above Stacks of vintage books are everywhere in Lynda's home, including in her bedroom. The aged pages and worn spines with their beautiful textures and faded colours, are a feature in themselves. **Opposite left** Lynda's large collection of paintings from the early 1900s is displayed in clusters around her home. The colour palette of the artworks complements her furnishings and textiles and contrasts well with her more industrial pieces. **Opposite right** This former mattress factory was once in bad shape but hard work and love have transformed it into a beautiful home.

Kabinett and Kammer

A curiosity shop of sorts, Kabinett and Kammer has been designed with a true artist's eye. The decor and the curation of the goods have combined to create a space in which a sense of eccentricity and masculinity shines through the layers of decoration on walls and surfaces to make a great visual feast.

the shop

It is no surprise that Sean Scherer, owner of Kabinett and Kammer, is first and foremost a fine artist. His shop, located in Andes, upstate New York, is in itself a work of art, as is Sean's home, the apartment above the shop. It seems that Sean lives and breathes beautiful, unique objects, as they fill every corner of his public and private spaces, and each one of these corners invites you to explore with your eyes and discover the stories within.

He has had a long-standing passion for objects with history, buying his first antique at the age of 16. His art education is intrinsically entwined with his current life as a shop owner. He says: 'My eye is trained as a contemporary artist and I choose objects for the store that interest me as an artist and can be displayed and appreciated as art on their own.'

Sean's life changed after the 9/11 attacks in New York. He witnessed the terrible events up close and suffered some residual trauma in the following years. His creativity affected, leaving him unable to paint, he took to renovating a farmhouse in upstate New York instead. During this time, he developed friendships with a community of creative minds in the area, and it was retired actress-turned-antiques dealer Brooke Alderson who encouraged Sean to open his shop in 2007.

Top *On some walls, Sean has used a dark charcoal grey paint, although he says he often changes the paint colour to suit his current stock.*

Bottom *The natural world, anatomy and typography are all strong themes here, reflecting the significance of the store's name, which is derived from the history of the cabinet of curiosities, or* Kunstkabinett *or* Wunderkammer.

Opposite *Some of the walls inside Kabinett and Kammer have been covered in pages from old book pages, prints and ephemera. It creates a completely unique look, which is intriguing both from afar and up close.*

the home

When Sean moved above the shop, there were two separate apartments. He knocked through to make one large space, then simply painted and installed antique lighting throughout. The floors are mostly painted white, although many rooms are warmed up with beautiful rugs. Walls are a pale, unimposing grey, creating an elegant backdrop for his collections.

The flamingo in the hallway is one of Sean's favourite pieces in his home, not only for its beauty, but also as it reminds him of home – Miami. It is just one small part of his taxidermy collection, which boasts a shark, a swan and an ostrich, to name a few. Well-loved, farmhouse-style wooden furniture sits happily alongside colourful glassware, an anatomical model of a human torso and art in gilt frames. The space feels fresh, but has lots of layers and texture. It is a carefully curated collection of unique objects, put together in a warm and welcoming way.

Sean spends a lot of time here styling vignettes for the shop, building stories around each object. His artist's eye allows him not just to display items but create mini masterpieces in every corner. His home is a stylish, beautiful and, above all, unique living space.

Above *The wall space by the staircase has been utilized fully for Sean's impressive art collection.*

Right *The walls are mainly painted pale grey, with floors in white, a subtle base to allow his unusual taxidermy artefacts to really stand out.*

Opposite *Sean is not shy when it comes to making bold statements in his home. His dining table is quietly observed by an anatomical model, and a 2m (7ft), ornate column stands proud in one corner.*

KABINETT AND KAMMER
7 Main Street, Andes, NY 13731, USA
www.kabinettandkammer.com

Inheritance

Vintage ceramics, old books and unexpected *objets d'art* cover every one of the the surfaces of this Los Angeles-based shop, where all aspects of the display has been carefully considered and impeccably styled for a 'masculine eclectic' aesthetic to create a visual surrpise around every corner.

the shop

Originally a set dresser and prop stylist, Michael Andrews began working at LA-based shop Zelen while he was a freelancer. When the owner, Dan Zelen, decided to move to San Francisco in 2009, Michael took over the reins of the shop, as he felt his style and aesthetic were akin to the look that Dan had created.

Michael continued to build on Dan's eclectic taste, but at the same time developed his own approach to curating the store, and after feeling that it had become 'his' shop, he changed the name to Inheritance. The new name reflects what Michael feels the store's contents are worthy of becoming; he hopes the vintage and modern collectibles and handcrafted wares he sells will be handed down to future generations for years to come.

Left *There is a lot to look at in eclectic shop Inheritance. It contains a collection of unusual and beautiful objects, which owner Michael hopes will stay in the buyer's family for generations – hence the store's name.*

Opposite *There is a richness to the space, owing to the choice of dark colour against carefully curated furniture and decorative items.*

Michael cites male designers such as Tony Duquette, Steven Gambrel and Gert Voorjans as being influential on how he decorates. His use of colour is striking yet allows objects to remain the focal point. Dark navy-painted shelving creates a strong background for a collection of colourful plates as well as other *objets d'art*. But otherwise the walls have been left an off-white, emphasizing the textured nature of the old loft's interior. The store's look is very layered – things on top of things – with textures weaving together for a rich, warm and inviting atmosphere. Michael admits that sometimes the layering can appear overwhelming, but he wanted to create the feel of a European flea market, where there is lots to explore and discover as the shopper makes their way around the space.

Still, the displays are well considered, because Michael believes the way that a customer perceives items in store will

Above Michael's stock is constantly evolving as most pieces are unique, but he strives to keep a cohesive look through careful styling.

Right The shop has a very layered look. As Michael says: 'Things on top of things, different textures weaving together, to create something rich.'

Opposite above and below Michael says he wanted to create the look of a European flea market or antique shop, but in his city of LA. While his displays are considered, they still allow the shopper to feel like they are having a good rummage.

influence whether they can live with them in their own home. It is a constantly evolving space that reflects his own taste shifts as well as the collectors he works with.

When decorating a large-scale space you can afford to be bold. Experiment with colour to create sections and add warmth. And lookout in salvage yards for fabulous larger decorative items or furniture you may otherwise not have considered in your home. These can help fill large spaces and also create talking points for your visitors.

the home

At home – an industrial warehouse in downtown LA, originally the home of Heinz 57 – Michael and his partner have continued the rich, layered theme, but in a more minimal way. The open-plan living space and high ceilings offered by such a converted building are perfect for introducing unusual large-scale items that would normally be unsuitable in a traditional home. Pieces such as a 4m- (13ft-) tall surveyor's tool, an enormous stag's head and enormous artworks are given room to breathe and are really a necessity to fill the wall and floor space.

Michael tends not to bring things home from the shop to use in his own home, and says that most of their possessions are an accumulation of things they had collected separately over the years. Luckily their two styles came together with ease. Vignettes and the use of grid-like formations for hanging art and collections of plates are a good solution for filling large wall expanses and create a pleasing symmetry.

Above In this spacious environment, Michael has created room-like zones within the space. Each zone preserves a sense of enclosure while forming an overall part of open-plan loft living. The result is a great eclectic mix.

Opposite The centrepiece in the kitchen is the large island, a repurposed retail shop display unit. As well as creating a large worktop for preparing meals, it also holds books and magazines in the clear drawers.

Above *Michael groups his collections of Fornasetti china together for maximum impact. The quirky plate designs make a strong display in a grid formation in his kitchen.*

Left *A large, open-plan loft space allows for a chunky dining table with comfy button-back chairs, plus a full-height, folding screen on wheels. Freestanding screens and half-height partitions, some decorated with wallpaper, form self-contained 'rooms' within the space.*

INHERITANCE
8055 Beverly Blvd., Los Angeles, CA 90048, USA
www.inheritanceshop.com

Homeware Shops

While shopping online is an easy and accessible way to decorate your home, there is nothing like discovering a hidden gem of a shop in a new city or walking into a store and breathing in the scent of a delicious candle burning. Not to mention the experience of actually touching the products, feeling the quality and really connecting with something that you know is perfect for your home.

Despite this, homewares stores do have to work harder these days to compete with the online marketplace, and it is something all our featured shop owners can identify with. They therefore strive to make their retail space one that has real heart and soul, and that will ensure that customers keep coming back.

RARE DEVICE (page 168) holds regular art events, which attract local creative clientele, while Sabine, owner of ROOM TO DREAM (page 158), is constantly transforming her store's appearance, offering a fresh look, new products and inspiration to her frequent visitors.

Whether your preference is modern, eclectic, handmade or Scandi, it is the job of these homewares purveyors to inspire you.

DECORATING IDEAS TO TAKE HOME WITH YOU FROM HOMEWARE SHOPS

1 Homewares do not have to be hidden away behind cupboard doors. Create a display from everyday objects with peg rails or miniature shelving and make a feature of your display.

2 Paper products are a cheap and easy way to add interest by hanging them from the ceiling or walls.

3 Dot colourful items of china or glass around a neutral display to create a jolt of colour on some shelving or on a tabletop.

Opposite Room to Dream, Munich, Germany

Effortlessly chic Scandi style reigns supreme at this Munich location. Bright, fresh and modern, Room to Dream will inspire a classic Nordic vibe while keeping you up to date with current trends.

the shop

Sabine Stadtherr has two passions in life: fashion and interior design. She initially followed a career in fashion after being offered a place at the Fashion Institute of Technology in New York, and spent 18 years working as a knitwear designer. But with her love of interiors ever present, in 2013 she decided to initiate a career change, and opened her shop, Room to Dream, in central Munich.

Despite being only a few steps away from the hustle and bustle of the main pedestrian zone, Room to Dream is surrounded by a calming oasis of trees, fountains and green space, with an ambience that is reflected when you step inside the store. Flooded with natural light from the large front window, the shop is bright and airy, and is filled with furnishings and accessories of mainly Nordic origin.

A lover of all things Scandinavian, Sabine says she is influenced by the Scandi way of life and the importance that a beautiful home holds for these Nordic dwellers. Good design and quality craftsmanship are central to her product range, and she stocks many classic pieces as well as her own Room to Dream line. While Sabine is very hot on current trends, and regularly attends furniture fairs to find out what is happening in the design world, her ethos is very much focused on how to combine old

and new looks. Rather than discarding last season's items and replacing them with the new – something she disliked about the fashion industry – she enjoys the challenge of blending the two. After each fair, she creates a large inspiration board in the shop where she pins colour swatches and products she plans to buy, and makes sure that these will fit with her existing stock. A clever idea, which could also be used at home when planning a refresh.

Above *The bright, airy space of Room to Dream's shop unit is the perfect environment for showing off Sabine's range of Scandinavian goods.*

Opposite *Sabine's in-store styling is impeccable. She has created inspiring room arrangements with clear colour schemes and lots of ideas for how to display her wares.*

Room to
Dream

the home

Sabine's home, situated around 30 minutes away from the city centre, is a two-storey maisonette (duplex) which she and her husband purchased ten years ago. Built in 1986, the complex comprises 36 apartments, all of which have different floor plans. Leaving the interesting architecture and features untouched, the couple merely removed a kitchen wall to create an open-plan space. The triangular windows, a mix of high and sloping ceilings and the impressive count of four balconies mean the apartment has lots of character, despite not being particularly old.

In her home, Sabine's goal was to create a space that made it easy and quick to unwind in. She's chosen a soft and neutral colour scheme, which she admits some might find boring, but for her it is more about paying attention to aspects such as texture: mixing chunky knitted cushions with soft leather ones, or combining coloured glassware with handmade ceramics.

The couple love the flexibility that the open-plan living area gives them, and they often move furniture around depending on how they are using the space. They can arrange it formally if having guests

Above Sabine loves furniture that is multi functional as well as stylish. This piece can be a cosy seat for two, or folded out into a comfortable bed when they have guests.

Opposite above Flexible seating is a real bonus if you are entertaining a crowd or having people to stay over.

Opposite below In the kitchen, a dramatic bowl and a colourful painting are used as simple decoration in this contemporary space.

Previous page Sabine and her husband love the open-plan living that their two-storey apartment offers. They often rearrange furniture to suit their specific needs. A relatively new building, the apartment still has lots of great features, including some triangular windows and interesting sloping lines.

over, or create a cosy nest if lounging by the fire. In fact, freedom of adjustability is something Sabine practises regularly at home and at her store. She is drawn to interchangeable furniture such as the stacking shelf system by Scandinavian brand Muuto, whose box sections can be stacked on top of each other, lined up alongside one other, or used singly as a side table. Although Sabine uses colour boldly in her shop – in the form of large boards that both disguise radiators and become a feature in their own right – at home she prefers a white backdrop, with moveable furniture and textural colour on paintings and soft furnishings, to provide visual interest.

ROOM TO DREAM
Lenbachplatz 7, 80333 Munich, Germany
www.room-to-dream.de

Brooklyn Slate

This store brings a hint of New England informality to the generous-sized industrial space in which it is housed. White wooden panelling contrasts beautifully with the raw brickwork and factory-style surfaces for a cool-laid-back interior that is both comfortable and welcoming.

the shop

Brooklyn Slate Company owners, Sean Tice and Kristy Hadeka, first discovered the versatility and popularity of slate after a visit to Kristy's family quarry in upstate New York, back in 2009. After taking some slate for use at home, they started gifting some to friends, and had an overwhelming response to what they had created with it. This encouraged them to develop a line of slate products for the home, and their business was born in 2010. The bricks and mortar shop opened its doors in 2013, and the pair have continued to source their slate from the family quarry, while creating the products themselves at their studio in Brooklyn.

The space they've designed for retailing their products draws inspiration from the white wood

Left *A New England vibe has been brought to the Brooklyn-based shop via white wood panelling and the floor-to-ceiling compartment shelving.*

Opposite above *The bare brick wall represents the building's industrial history and contrasts well with the fresh white paint on the shelving and payment counter.*

Opposite below *Sean loves having plants in the store, and often changes them with the season. This is a clever idea for filling the recess in the brick wall here.*

panelling common to New England interiors. The store is located in the Red Hook area of Brooklyn, just a few blocks from the 19th-century piers and boat basins, so they have incorporated a subtle nautical theme, mixing this with the building's industrial look. Large windows, exposed brick and old factory lighting, contrast well with the crisp white panelling and sleek wooden furniture.

A selection of potted plants creates a feature nestled in the brick wall on one side of the store. Sean explains that they tend to adhere to a constant aesthetic, but introduce new ideas each season. Window displays are updated every few months, and seasonal plants are generally used to freshen the look.

Displays are minimal and ordered without being clinical. Their slate products are neatly spaced and lined up on the hairpin leg table and benches and framed in the grid-style shelving. All the pieces are tied with twine and a brown paper branded label, adding to the handmade, rustic design.

the home

Sean and Kristy's preference for minimal interiors carries over to their home: a ground-floor apartment in a traditional New York brownstone. The building itself is typical of these turn-of-the-century terrace (row) houses – wooden floors throughout, beautiful stamped tin ceilings and tall windows. The couple painted everywhere white, adhering to their classic, simple style, but added open shelving in the living area and kitchen. Books, photos and kitchenware displayed here add character and colour to the otherwise uncluttered spaces.

Of the objects, textiles and artwork the couple own, most are gathered from their travels abroad, and while they have a few design stores they occasionally shop at, a lot of their furniture has been designed and built by themselves. One of their favourite pieces is a floating entertainment shelf beneath the television. It is a simple design solution to the problem of unsightly cables, as it hides them all away in a subtle and stylish way. Their dining table is a reflection of their shop furniture choices: a simple hairpin-leg design, accompanied by sleek Eames dining chairs.

Of course some of their own slate products can be found in their home, along with a few other items they stock, such as enamel cups in the kitchen. The store sells a range of additional goods that complement Sean and Kristy's slate range – mainly cheese-related items, as well as a carefully selected collection of recipe books and magazines. They have created a lifestyle around the natural material they have chosen to work with, not only through beautifully made products but also the interior aesthetic that surrounds them. A perfect balance has been found between the handmade, rustic appearance of the slate and the minimalism of the space. It is evident the duo are hugely influenced by architect and interior designer Frank Lloyd Wright.

Left The typical features of a Brooklyn brownstone, such as the windows, exposed brick walls and wooden floors, speak for themselves in the bedroom. Simple, fresh decor and modern furniture work well here, as does a quirky, wall-mounted deer's head.

Opposite Eames chairs and a hairpin table, similar to those used in Brooklyn Slate, create a simple, yet stylish dining area. The home has a neutral, minimal aesthetic, with colour introduced via abstract art, their book collection, photos and souvenirs, all adding a personal touch.

BROOKLYN SLATE
305 Van Brunt Street, Brooklyn, NY 11231, USA
www.brooklynslate.com

Rare Device

A native North American tree, a manzanita, forms an eye-catching centrepiece in the Rare Device store, but the airy space is otherwise completely pared back, to allow the contemporary yet playful collection of goods speak for themselves.

the home

'It was a miracle of rare device', a line from the Samuel Taylor Coleridge poem *Kubla Khan*, describing the pleasure dome created by the Mongol emperor, that inspired the name of the San Francisco shop owned by Giselle Gyalzen.

Rare Device celebrates its tenth anniversary in 2015, having had a very interesting first decade.

Giselle took over the business in 2011 having abandoned a job in advertising after hearing the news that owners Rena Tom and Lisa Congdon were moving on. She leapt at the chance to fulfil her dream of owning a shop, and now she has two in San Francisco, where she holds regular art shows and events which are enjoyed by local creatives.

Giselle took inspiration from the original store she had taken over when it came to designing her new location on Divisadero Street (pictured here). The old shop front was painted blue, so she chose

to paint the floor in the same shade, but kept the walls and shelving white, as her merchandise was colourful and bold. To catch the eye of shoppers, Giselle painted the door yellow and the floor blue.

On the shelves, customers will find an eclectic selection of goods, chosen for their beauty, usefulness and craftsmanship. From ceramics and stationery to illustrative artwork and printed textiles, the locally sourced products, as well as how they are displayed, are extremely important to Giselle.

Above *Colourful contemporary cabinets are used for storing products but also create a bright, cheerful display area.*

Opposite *Simple and bold graphic styling gives the store clean, contemporary lines in keeping with the products themselves.*

the home

When she's not busy with Rare Device, Giselle enjoys family life with her husband and their two children back home in the Bernal Heights area of the city. Their two-bedroom apartment has breathtaking views of San Francisco, making it a wonderful place to unwind and relax. When the couple moved in eight years ago, it was in great condition, so there was no need to carry out much work to the place. They simply painted and set about making it a comfortable home for their family.

The main living space is open-plan, combining cooking, eating and relaxing in one space. The colourful, whimsical and modern feel of Rare Device is mirrored here, with bright textiles mixing with classic furniture design and contemporary lighting. The corner reserved for dining also includes

a comfy window seat, which is a favourite spot for observing those panoramic city vistas. The elevated location also means they witness many natural manifestations such as stunning sunsets, low fog lines and full, double rainbows.

The couple have opted for an uncluttered environment with clean lines, but have added fun, design elements, such as the floating shelves in the living area and the quirky artwork displayed in the

Above left A vibrant red-painted display cabinet houses everyday china, combining storage and display close to the kitchen/dining area.

Above right Open-plan living works perfectly for Giselle and her family of four. They can cook, eat and socialize together in this contemporary space.

Opposite A panoramic view over San Francisco is the perfect scene to enjoy over breakfast each morning. Giselle has mixed contemporary and traditional design along with fun, colourful cushions on the window seat.

children's bedroom. Many pieces in their home are stocked at Rare Device, although generally Giselle restrains herself from bringing home too much from the shop, preferring to occasionally select one-of-a-kind pieces from the gallery shows that they host.

The home and shop both have a strong sense of style, despite not being particularly influenced by one specific era or look. In fact, lots of different styles are at play here – a mix of mid-century seating, French country cabinets and contemporary storage solutions. The beautifully edited end result is testament to Giselle's ability to fuse these looks together stylishly, creating fresh, comfortable and inspiring spaces.

Above A colourful graphic canvas tones in with the blue-coloured upholstery that brings this neutral space to life.

Opposite Giselle allows aspects of family life to be visible by incorporating her children's toys and artwork into the space, while still keeping it super-stylish and tidy.

RARE DEVICE
600 Divisadero St., San Francisco, CA 94117, USA
www.raredevice.net

Cafe Shops

One of my favourite things to do when indulging in a little retail therapy is to stop for a sit-down, a cuppa and a slice of cake! So what could be more perfect than a shop with a cafe inside? The good news is that multi-functional venues are becoming more prevalent, and whether it is the result of retailers simply adding more strings to their bow or whether some have identified the benefits of such a combination, it is certainly something I am happy to see.

Some, such as LE ROCKETSHIP in Paris, have opted for a small coffee bar. Here, owner Benoît can socialize with his customers, sharing with them his passion for the products he sells and the makers he works with. Others, such as London's

DRINK SHOP & DO, have chosen to make their cafe/bar the dominant aspect of the venue, incorporating a small shop area as well as selling all the furniture and china used in the cafe. Whatever the arrangement, it is certainly difficult to leave empty-handed, as your cake-fuelled pit stop gives you time to convince yourself to buy that must-have tea towel, or the Formica table you dined at.

DECORATING IDEAS TO TAKE HOME WITH YOU FROM CAFE SHOPS

1 Cafes are good places to inspire your choice of china and tableware, whether vintage or modern.

2 Look at how the furniture is put together and why it works – is it a collection of mismatched and painted chairs or a mix of zinc-topped tables and antique pieces?

3 Get inspiration for your table settings from the way food is presented and served. And check out the flowers and vases. Often simplicity works well.

Opposite Drink, Shop & Do, UK

Le Rocketship

A top tip for coffee lovers when in Paris: Le Rocketship is the perfect pit stop for caffeine, accompanied by a helping of inspiration for your home. Owner Benoît is meticulous in his product selection and visual merchandising, telling a story with every piece of display in the shop.

the shop

As Benoît Touche approached his 40th birthday, he decided that he needed to make a dramatic change to his professional life. After years of working in marketing and communications, he was feeling unfulfilled and stressed. He strongly felt the need to live by his own rules and to follow his dreams. The result of this soul-searching was Le Rocketship, a shop selling lifestyle products, artwork and books, with the addition of a small coffee bar.

When considering the concept behind his business, Benoît quotes from the Japanese interiors book *Lifecycling*; a fellow shop owner based in Los Angeles says: 'a big part of my store's philosophy comes from the way I lived my whole adult life. I'm interested by things that have permanence'. This idea resonates strongly with Benoît, not only with the fact that it is a way of life for him, but that he personally seeks out items of lasting quality and skilful craftsmanship that have a story to tell. And what better way to retell these stories than over a great cup of coffee. Benoît wanted to include a coffee bar within the store, making it a destination to not only shop, but to relax and chat. Never one to do things by halves, Benoît trained as a barista and did extensive research into the art of coffee-making to ensure he was supplying a high-quality product that was of the same calibre of merchandise in his store.

Left *Le Rocketship stocks a hand-picked selection of lifestyle products, from art books and stationery to ceramics and furniture.*

Opposite *Benoît takes the coffee aspect of Le Rocketship very seriously, aspiring to serve some of the best coffee in Paris.*

This corner of the store has a distinctly graphic aesthetic. Art and photography books are stacked neatly, while Benoît has used the 'rule of three' to display typographical prints along the walls.

Benoît spends a lot of time curating his collection, ensuring that everything works together visually, sometimes even tying together their back stories via the displays. Plants feature heavily too – something else he has a great passion for.

the home

Moving here in 2006, Benoît and his family made the conscious decision to live in a modern building after their previous home, an older property, caused constant problems. They wanted not only a larger space, but one that simply required them to fill it with their possessions and personality. Their main living space is open-plan, incorporating their kitchen, dining area and living room. Dominating one wall is a large bookcase, built by Atelier 154, a Parisian furniture-maker. The design was inspired by the work of Charlotte Perriand, a 20th-century French designer, and is not only a functional piece of furniture but a great example of craftsmanship. The large, farm-style dining table was a 30th birthday gift, another sturdy and timeless piece that is only getting

better with age. The table is flanked by a mismatched selection of classic vintage chairs, some with splashes of red, which tie in the look with the red panels of the bookcase. They spent a long time searching for the perfect piece of art to hang above the table, and it eventually came in the form of a beautiful collage work by a French artist, which creates a bold and graphic statement when looking back across the living-dining room.

Large glass doors that open on to the balcony flood the space with natural light, and Benoît's favourite greenery is displayed on open shelving.

LE ROCKETSHIP
13 bis rue Henry Monnier, 75009 Paris, France
www.lerocketship.com

Opposite Benoît's family home is also full of many stories about each and every item contained within it. Honeymoon souvenirs, birthday gifts and sought-after artwork are all form a part of the family's history. **Above** Benoît has many items from the shop in his home, in fact he says that his home inspired the shop. Here he has hung typographical prints in the same way as he has done in the store. His love of houseplants is clearly evident.

Drink, Shop & Do

Drink, Shop & Do will indulge your taste buds and your creativity simultaneously. The decor at this colourful north London venue is the result of the proprietor's lifelong love of flea markets. Retro tables, mismatched chairs, china and glassware are cool, not quaint, and are a visual treat in this trendy spot.

the shop

Drink, Shop & Do is a multifunctional venue, located in the regenerated Kings Cross area of north London. Through the front door, a small shop area stocks quirky gifts, homewares, vintage finds and craft supplies. Further on, steps lead to the main cafe/bar area, where high ceilings and a skylight allow light to pour in. Everything in the cafe is for sale – from the mismatched vintage chairs to the salt and pepper shakers and glass decanters.

Joint owners Kristie Bishop and Coralie Sleap opened Drink, Shop & Do in 2009. As old school friends, they discovered over a cup of tea one day that they had similar dreams for a business, so decided to join forces. Both lovers of vintage, they chose to source second-hand furniture and tableware to fill the space. Their start-up budget was small, so this suited perfectly. They found many of their items at car boot sales, thrift shops and the occasional flea market in France. Over the years they say they've had to become more thoughtful and practical when hunting for goods for the cafe, as, unfortunately,

Left *Shop while you dine at Drink, Shop & Do. Everything you sit on, eat from and pour milk from is for sale. Kristie is continually sourcing furniture and accessories from flea markets, so the space changes regularly as items are sold and replaced.*

Above Coloured Formica tables are flanked by a collection of mismatched vintage chairs, filling this historical London building. Lots of the original features are beautifully preserved, including the ornate columns and domed ceiling.

items do get broken easily. Kristie admits that she tends to keep her favourite finds at home, as it would be too upsetting to see them get damaged in the shop.

The building itself has a very colourful history. Originally a Victorian Turkish bath, it has since been a brothel, a rave venue in the 1980s, a sex shop and an art gallery. Today, the fun is much cleaner; with activities such as tea towel screen-printing or jewellery-making taking place, but the architecture is a reminder of the building's age, with its beautiful columns, cornicing and a domed ceiling in the back room.

the home

Kristie's love of the past is apparent in her home too. She has renovated her four-bedroom Edwardian terrace (row) house in south west London, creating a modern home in an old building, and mixing her extensive vintage china collection with contemporary artwork and colourful textiles.

Her country-style kitchen has many similarities with Drink, Shop & Do, and she says the two have inspired each other. A wide variety of teas in glass canisters are lined up on open shelving; mismatched vintage china and glassware are displayed in a glass-fronted cabinet; and a set of old wooden chairs has been given an update with floral fabric.

Kristie has noticed that being a shop owner has influenced how she displays items in her home. She finds she groups things in threes or more, and most things that she owns multiples of – a collection of 35 teacups and 27 blankets – prove this theory. Graphic

prints in her kitchen and sitting room are hung in triptychs, each group created by the same artist, almost like a matching set. Many of the items she stocks in the shop often find their way into her home too; she admits it's easy to add on an extra unit when placing wholesale orders.

In both retail and residential spaces, Kristie has used a plain backdrop of crisp white or calming grey and injects colour with accessories and furnishings. As everything in the cafe is for sale, she has to keep a stock of vintage chairs, tables and crockery to replace

Left Vintage wooden chairs re-covered in vintage fabric bring informality to the dining table, above which hang vintage posters that bring some cohesive colour to the otherwise neutral room.

any that are sold, so the aesthetic is constantly changing. But this is something she does naturally at home too, changing her interior with the seasons, usually in April and October, by updating art on the walls, adding or taking away soft furnishings and repositioning items.

Similar to having a summer and winter wardrobe, Kristie's idea stops your interior from becoming stagnant and is a fun way of welcoming a new season with either spring brights or warm, winter textiles.

Above *Exposed brickwork and kitchen units painted off-white create warmth in this cosy, but simple, country-style kitchen.*

Opposite above *A built-in dresser unit gives plenty of room for Kristie to display her collection of vintage teapots and china cups.*

DRINK, SHOP & DO
9 Caledonian Road, London N1 9DX, UK
www.drinkshopdo.com

Outdated

Design periods mix seamlessly at this upstate New York cafe and store. Here you may enjoy your cake on a retro 1970s plate, while sitting on a 1950s chair at a 100-year-old table. This varied vintage store champions a 'buy what you love' ethos and strives for an eclectic look throughout the space.

the shop

It was a shared love of antiques and good coffee that led Gabriel Constantine and Tarah Gay to open Outdated, their shop and restaurant venue. When the couple first met, they loved taking road trips to search out great shops and the best places to drink coffee and eat. They dreamt of a space that catered for both of these pastimes, where jars of cookies were for sale next to jars of pins; where you could spend a small amount of money on a hot cup of coffee or a lot more on a beautiful old farm table. They dreamt of a place where they could combine their love of food and antiques and create somewhere that people could enjoy and feel at home.

Since opening their store in 2012, the couple have stayed true to their sense of style. Their eclectic look is created by the combination of design periods – from Victorian to contemporary. They prefer the aesthetic of an old rustic table teamed with sleek Herman Miller chairs rather than a set of 'matching' chairs. Their theory is that 'if we love something, it usually works with our other loved stuff'.

They are passionate about buying for and styling their shop and would never trust the job to anyone else. They try to source locally as much as possible, for both the cafe and the shop, and recently have

even stocked some vintage dry goods, which was old inventory from one of their catering suppliers. They look everywhere for opportunities to buy furniture and fittings, from an old hardware close by to a hotel that is closing down further afield.

They've always got their eyes and ears open for buying opportunities and design possibilities. On a weekly basis they find themselves out and about hunting for treasures, frequenting many auctions, discovering antique stores and walking on the beach to turn up beautiful feathers or shells, perfect for displaying in their home. They love geological forms and one of their favourite places to seek inspiration is their local Museum of Natural History.

Above *Outdated combines good cuisine and a passion for antiques.*

Right *A comfy chair offers a home from home in this cafe store.*

Opposite *A varied and eclectic range of vintage goods, from colourful Indian archery arrows to paint palettes and metal travelling trunks, sits well together, linked by colour and material.*

__Above__ Rarely buying new, the couple love to group together similar items such as these vintage desk bells.

__Left__ They love the texture of old wood, so use it a lot in their home. Glass domes are a beautiful and practical way to display delicate antique taxidermy.

__Opposite__ The home is an eclectic mix of periods – a 1930s club chair, Victorian bird domes and a painted apothecary chest all reside comfortably in the living room The differing materials and textures create a layered, tactile aesthetic, similar to a cosy log cabin.

__Previous page__ Gabriel and Tarah's kitchen mixes rustic farmhouse with industrial factory, for a warm, inviting space with lots of character.

the home

There is a very obvious crossover between the couple's home and their shop. They try hard to present their stock in ways that inspire customers to style their own homes, including fun ideas for serving food, using mismatched plates, old wooden boxes for cutlery (silverware) or wire baskets for table linens. Their love for old wood with lots of patina is evident in both spaces, with the use of bright fabrics to add colour. Many items from the shop can be spotted around their home. They admit that one of the perks of being a shop owner is how it allows you to streamline what you own. They can sell items that perhaps no longer work in their home, as they fit seamlessly into the shop surroundings.

Gabriel and Tarah say their home is in a constant state of flux; there is always scope to improve it, change it, better use it. While a home is a place to feel safe, nurtured and familiar, they enjoy the element of surprise and the feeling of freshness a change can create – a little bit like life itself. They surround themselves with things they love, that hold memories and that inspire them, and they hope that the retail space they have created may have the same effect on the visitors that spend time there.

OUTDATED
314 Wall St., Kingston, NY 12401, USA
www.facebook.com/outdatedcafe

Craft Shops

With a monumental revival of the crafting scene in recent years, haberdasheries and craft supply stores have experienced a boom period, with many fabulous new venues opening to feed the hunger for beautiful fabrics, designer yarns and even stylish scissors. These ateliers have contributed to the hip new image associated with modern makers, firstly by stocking the most desirable of supplies, and secondly housing them in spaces that ooze inspiration, not only for your next craft project, but for your home too.

Often, painted vintage furniture and fittings are used for storage and display, along with geometric wall-mounted display units that would be great ideas for storing your own yarn collection, while custom built-in furniture or old apple crates are good as shelving.

Whether you're a crafty type or not, you can still gather ideas from

these homespun spaces, as well as getting inspiration from how the

owners have incorporated their love of making into their homes.

Even if you don't enjoy sewing, knitting or paper crafts, many of

the supplies and tools of the trade are great for styling your home.

DECORATING IDEAS TO TAKE HOME WITH YOU FROM CRAFT SHOPS

1 Grade your crafts supplies by size, colour or material and assess how much storage space you will need for each.

2 The most effective solution is often a combination of pigeonholes or some form of open storage, along with drawers and wall-mounted pieces.

3 Sand down and repaint vintage storage units, adding new door handles or glass knobs for a cohesive decorative effect.

Opposite The Old Haberdashery, UK

Sew Over It

This bright and airy sewing cafe and shop uses a signature colour to punctuate the mainly white space. Second-hand finds have been repurposed to furnish the shop, as well as to display the colourful crafting supplies perfectly.

the shop

When Lisa Comfort opened her first sewing cafe and shop in 2011, she wanted to create an inspiring space where crafters could come to work either independently or with the guidance of an expert. The interior, therefore, was hugely important, as it needed to be preferential to the customer's home, where most people tend to spend their crafting time. Lisa put a lot of effort into making a welcoming and homey environment, and says she is constantly editing and changing the space a little to keep it interesting for regulars. The supply of tea and cake is of course an added enticement to visit.

Vibrant chairs in the signature Sew Over It blue surround a group of work tables, each with a pretty teapot filled with flowers and a collection of sewing essentials. Shelves are neatly lined with jars of buttons, zips and fasteners, with everything for sale and meticulously labelled – almost like the crafter's equivalent of an old-fashioned sweet shop or candy store. The large windows flood the bright white space with light – perfect conditions for intricate sewing

work – and reams of colourful fabric are lined up ready to be transformed into a beautiful dress or a pair of curtains. A vintage wall unit which has been upcycled, painted white with cute blue and red drawer handles, now houses a rainbow of yarns, and to top it off, a colourful glass chandelier bought online gives an added burst of fun to the space.

To further inspire, examples of what can be created are dotted around the shop on mannequins. Lisa's passion is dressmaking, so many of the classes are geared towards this, and she also stocks a range of Sew Over It patterns to work from or take home. The fabrics she carries come from all over the world, from Hong Kong to Italy to India. In fact, it was just after a trip to India that she bought her most favourite item, now in her London home: a bright turquoise blue mirror.

Above left Lisa found this unit at Sunbury Antiques Market in Surrey, UK. It had been in an old barn for a long time, and there was a spider in every drawer! She spruced it up with white paint and some colourful knobs. *Above right* Sew Over It is a colourful shop, and Lisa's choice of lighting fits in perfectly. The bold chandelier is a fun, slightly eccentric feature. *Opposite* Homespun-style blinds (shades) hang in the window of Sew Over It, while wooden furniture, painted by Lisa in her signature blue colour pops out against the white walls and woodwork.

Left *Lisa's lounge has a strong blue theme, mixing shades, patterns and textures. She has even managed to introduce vintage pieces with scuffed blue surfaces.*

Below *The stairs in Lisa's London home have been given a fun update using wallpaper on the risers.*

Opposite *In the bedroom, contemporary lighting contrasts with vintage furniture, while colours have been kept subtle and calming.*

the home

In Lisa's home, blue is a strong accent colour, particularly in the living area. A centrepiece rug in varying shades of blue ties the different items together, from throws and cushions to a patterned upholstered chair, to the blue-tinged patina on a beautiful old trunk. Even the fireplace surround has been painted in a darker navy blue to complement the brighter shades. It is all set against a neutral palette of white and grey, making the blue theme a feature of the room without it being overpowering. Lisa enjoys the calming atmosphere the room exudes in comparison to her shop, which is more colourful and busy, but she says she couldn't live without the uplifting, energizing feeling that colour evokes in her.

The property, dating from 1900, has many classic period features such as a large arched doorway to the living room, wall panelling and beautiful banisters in the stairway. Lisa has kept the integrity of these features but modernized the space by adding fun elements such as bright retro wallpaper by Miss Print to the risers of the stairs. Her love of colour continues through to the kitchen where a collection of brightly patterned ceramics and vintage tins are displayed on open shelving. A set of four colourful baskets, which Lisa bought at a market in Delhi, are in grid formation on the wall – a storage solution that has become a feature in itself.

The calming colour palette of the sitting room is reflected in the bedroom. The bed is framed with an exposed brick wall, and its rough texture contrasts well with the more delicate painted antique painted furniture. The room is elegant and fuss-free but simple touches such as an old copy of *The Great Gatsby,* and pretty roses bring femininity to the space.

Both Lisa's home and shop have an airy feeling, allowing her love of patterned fabric and colour to shine. A sense of organization – a great asset to a sewer – is also evident in both places.

SEW OVER IT
78 Landor Road, London SW9 9PH, UK
www.sewoverit.co.uk

This quaint shop displays haberdashery goods amongst vintage finds and uses pieces from the past as clever display solutions. Every corner is picture-perfect, thanks to creative vignettes of sewing notions, haberdashery and vintage curios.

the shop

The well-travelled owner and creative mind behind The Old Haberdashery had an intriguing journey to opening up her shop in 2012. Sonia Boriczewski, a graduate in knitted textiles from the renowned Chelsea College of Art in London, spent five years teaching textiles and fashion history in Shanghai. This was followed by four years in Barcelona before returning to the UK.

Settling into family life in the Sussex countryside, Sonia's need to express her creativity was inherent. Her favourite pastime while living in Shanghai was foraging in antique markets for beautiful old textiles, vintage furniture and curios, and it was this activity, coupled with her love for crafting, that inspired her shop. After testing the water selling at local fairs, Sonia was soon ready to create her own retail space, selling a range of haberdashery notions alongside a carefully curated selection of vintage finds.

Sonia describes her shop as 'her open workshop, a place to create and place of ideas'. Her objective was to create a space where visitors would not only come to shop but to gather inspiration. It was her own childhood summers spent in Slovenia on her grandmother's farm that gave Sonia a taste for the eclectic. The farmhouse attic was filled with old but

well-loved objects, which she rummaged through often to see what delights she could uncover. This, along with her global travel experiences, plus her love of colour and textiles, has led to the diverse yet modern style of her store.

While the shop is a compact space, each area is styled as a carefully composed vignette. Grouping colours together, such as vibrant blue cotton reels (thread spools) with white and blue ceramic buttons and vases, keeps a coherence among what could otherwise appear cluttered. The walls and floor have been kept plain, in bright white, creating a blank canvas against which to set her vignettes.

Above *The Old Haberdashery is a treasure-trove of vintage china, glassware and of course sewing paraphernalia. A glass-fronted cabinet holds much of Sonia's most delicate items.*

Opposite *Sonia has repurposed an old workshop bench to display her wares, as well as utilizing wooden crates, vintage drawers and zinc buckets as interesting containers.*

The Old
Haberdashery

the home

Sonia's years spent in the Far East and occasional buying trips have heavily influenced her style preferences. However, this is much more evident in her own home. Sonia describes her two spaces as a bit like ying and yang – her shop being colourful and eclectic, while her home is pared back and tranquil. But she says the thread that ties the two together is the history and stories behind the items she collects.

Sonia's flair for grouping and displaying items continues in her home, although it has a very different feel. The colour scheme is generally neutral and subtle, and the vignettes of her glassware and Asian artefacts are more rustic in style. A friend once named her home the 'Asian cottage', describing the juxtaposition between the 17th-century English labourer's cottage and the treasures from her travels that fill the rooms within.

The interior characteristics are indicative of such a property – an abundance of bare, dark wood, including beams, and a slight lack of natural light. Sonia has worked hard to be sympathetic to the building in her decoration, but she has also counterbalanced these traits by using light colours on the walls, adding mirrors to reflect light and textiles to soften the hard aesthetic of the wood.

Many of her treasured possessions are those she found in the markets of Shanghai – a medicine chest in the bedroom, which has been restored, and her collection of Chinese textiles. These fabrics are so precious that she constantly moves them around to prevent them from fading and often packs them away for a while to help preserve the fibres. Her passion for textiles clearly informs all of her colour and design choices.

THE OLD HABERDASHERY
33 High Street, Ticehurst, East Sussex TN5 7AS, UK
www.theoldhaberdashery.com

Above Sonia's 17th-century cottage has an Asian flavour, reflecting the period of her life spent living in China. ***Opposite left*** Small wall-mounted shelves are perfect for displaying travel souvenirs and other precious possessions. Use items of varying heights and shapes, linked by a similar colour palette. ***Opposite right*** Embroidery threads, buttons and beads look wonderful displayed in glass jars.

Black Oveja

Upcycling and handmade ideas mix beautifully with a contemporary look in this Madrid-based haberdashery. Uniformity and order are key to the neat, innovative displays, while cute do-it-yourself ideas and mismatched furniture add an element of fun throughout this quirky and inviting store.

the shop

Black Oveja's logo is a visual hint to the shop name – Black Sheep – a Spanglish phrase chosen by owner Maria Mercedes Grosso. While attending design fairs and showing her clothing designs, Maria used to knit to pass the time. Visitors often asked if she taught knitting and so one day she thought: why not? Maria and Alfonso, her husband and business partner, quickly applied their strong sense of design to their store aesthetic. Here, they've created clever, practical and cohesive display solutions with a few fun design elements thrown in.

Custom-built furniture makes good use of space as well as housing fabric. Its bare wood adds to the recycled look and mixes well with the painted furniture and crates that are repurposed into shelving for the yarn collection. In the workshop area, examples of handmade garments are hung from simple clothes pegs attached to a long piece of wood – a budget-friendly yet super-stylish idea. Hexagonal wall shelving has a modern, architectural feel, and completes the juxtaposition of old and new within the store.

Top *Craft supplies and fabrics look great displayed in hexagonal wall units, built-in shelving and drawers with mismatched handles.*

Left *An easy DIY idea using a long piece of wood and clothes pegs creates a lovely way to hang up favourite pieces of clothing and artwork.*

Above *The Black Oveja sign.*

Opposite *A rainbow of yarns makes a colourful display in the corner of Black Oveja's Madrid store. Some are stacked in old wooden crates, others in custom made shelving.*

Next page *The home of Maria Mercedes Grosso exudes cool, calm Scandinavian-inspired influences.*

the home

The couple's home, an apartment not too far from their shop, also mixes modern pieces with recycled elements and vintage finds. Scandinavian style influences their dining area, with some original Eames chairs and a 1950s Danish table, while a small collection of teapots sits atop a modern sideboard. In contrast to their retail space, with its rainbow palette of yarns and fabrics, their home has a relatively neutral colour scheme. But it is clear Maria has an eye for colour, as pops of watermelon pink, turquoise blue and mint green have created a subtle theme throughout the space. Maria says Madrid is a city lacking in green space, and her upbringing in tropical Venezuela, means she has a yearning for greenery. A collection of houseplants in cute pots contributes a touch of nature, softening some of the more angular lines created by modern furniture and display units.

Top Similar to the shelving in Black Oveja, these crates on the couple's balcony at home makes for a cute, compact garden. ***Above*** In their bright living room, a basket of yarn and a sewing supplies box sit next to the sofa, hinting at Maria's crafty life. She has even coordinated the colours with the room! ***Opposite*** Clean, perpendicular lines are softened with a collection of houseplants, all potted in cute, quirky containers.

BLACK OVEJA
Calle de Sagasta, 7, 28004 Madrid, Spain
www.blackoveja.com

Loop

A colour-lovers dream, this crafter's haven is filled with yarns in every shade, delightfully displayed upon retro and vintage furniture of all shapes and sizes. The welcoming space, over two floors, has a cosy, homespun vibe, contrasting with the ornate, formal architectural details of the old building in which it is housed.

the shop

Light streams through the large window that greets you as you approach Loop, along London's quirky Camden Passage, enhancing the rainbow of colour that hits your eyes as you step inside. Shelves, baskets and boxes are crammed full of yarn in every shade and hue, and it is hard not to be inspired by the possibilities of what you could create from such a plethora of crafting supplies.

Susan Cropper, owner of Loop, opened her shop ten years ago in a response to a lack of retailers in London offering the great fibres and textiles that were in demand from the knitting community at the time. The style of the shop's interior hasn't changed much since opening. Susan has added and tweaked things here and there to make it easier for customers to navigate and she occasionally updates it with vintage finds she collects from around the world. An avid traveller, she is always on the lookout for things to add to the shop or to her own home, but in fact it is often on Loop's own doorstep where she picks up some of her best second-hand items. Camden Passage is host to a flea market twice a week, and is surrounded by a number of other antique shops – great sources for gathering display solutions for the shop's yarns, ribbons, buttons and threads.

Above *Loop is located next to one of London's best flea markets and surrounded by antique shops, a perfect spot for owner Susan to pick up vintage fittings for the store.*

Opposite *Retro furniture is used to display and store an extensive range of yarns. This corner looks cosy enough to curl up in with your knitting.*

Left *A pinboard above your workspace is great for pinning inspiration, reminders and for getting paperwork off the desk.*

Below *Incorporate your craft tools into your decor, like Susan has done here, with a pitcher filled with knitting needles.*

the home

Susan's home of nine years is across town. She is lucky that the old mansion block housing her apartment has maintained many of the original features and is blessed with stunning views of north London. Her biggest investment was the oiled oak floors throughout, but she is generally thrifty when it comes to gathering furnishings and decorative items. She often rescues pieces of furniture from the street, which have been discarded, and occasionally attends auctions in pursuit of a bargain. As well as being the proprietor of Loop, Susan also runs an online boutique (swoon-lounge.com) selling vintage homewares, so her quest for wonderful second-hand objects is very much a lifestyle, although she admits that many items in her home are 'stolen stock',

destined for Swoon's web pages, only to be pilfered for her personal use.

One such item, now hanging in her entrace hall, is among her most treasured: a two-sided painting she came across while visiting upstate New York. One side is a picture of a lake; the other, a woman sitting at a sewing machine near a window. The latter is her favourite, and she says the subject matter sums up so much in her life - textiles, Loop, her East Coast American heritage, memories of a road trip in New York and her new adventure with Swoon. At home, a soft colour palette creates a cosy sophistication.

LOOP
15 Camden Passage, Islington, London N1 8EA, UK
www.loopknitting.com

Don't be shy about creating a picture gallery on a wallpapered wall. Here, china plates and a mixture of other art have been layered on top of botanical-inspired wallpaper for a delicate, pretty look.

Adeline Klam

Bright colour and pattern burst from this store situated on a wide Parisian boulevard. Adeline is a paper crafting expert, and her shop demonstrates the beauty of decorating with paper, from origami garlands and tissue pompoms to paper flowers and fans.

the shop

In the 11th arrondissement of Paris is a shop that lovers of paper craft might just call heaven. Reams of Japanese paper line the walls, garlands of origami birds hang from the ceiling, and delicate flowers made of tissue paper sit atop shelves. Adeline Klam's colourful displays could well have you rummaging for hours as inspiration pours from this pretty shop.

Originally the store was solely a work studio, but after hanging her paper creations in the window, which faced onto the street, interest in what Adeline was doing grew, so she started to open up as a shop a few days a week. Today, six years on, she has a large retail space where she showcases a vast range of papers, fabrics, decorations, craft and party supplies. At the back of the shop, large glass panels separate a space from the shop where creative workshops in origami are held for both adults and children.

The spacious store feels airy and bright; Adeline chose to keep the walls and display units in neutral white so as to highlight the vast array of colours and patterns that fill the shelves and walls. All the furniture was designed and custom-made to fit her range of goods and she has added lots of handmade decorations created from the materials she stocks.

Above House-shaped display boxes and cute garlands decorate the wall behind Adeline's shop counter – an idea that could translate perfectly to a child's bedroom.

Left There's no doubt that flowers add that extra special something to any room – but if you can't afford to keep up a supply of fresh ones, then why not make some delightful tissue paper versions? Adeline has placed hers in simple glass bottles for a super-cute trio.

Opposite Adeline Klam's store is a pretty world of Japanese papers, washi tapes and crafting kits. The feminine colour palette against the white walls and fittings is fresh and endearing.

Adeline and her husband created a double-height ceiling in their central Paris apartment. Sometimes, if you lack in square footage, it is possible to gain space upwards.

the home

Just a few streets away from the store is Adeline's equally colourful home, which she shares with her husband and young son. Located on the top floor of an old building, the apartment is compact but has a feeling of openness and space due to the double-height ceiling in the living area. When the couple moved in eight years ago, they carried out extensive work and reclaimed the loft space to give height to the room. Wooden panelling was added to the ceiling to create the impression of a cute cottage in the heart of Paris.

As in the shop, tailor-made storage solutions were installed to maximize the small space, including the partition that separates the living room and kitchen. Built-in cupboards, drawers and open shelves, as well

as brightly painted sliding doors, house kitchenware, books and trinkets. Again, the majority of the walls and floors are painted in crisp white to allow Adeline to layer on colour and pattern. Fabric panels conceal any unsightly items, such as the television and computer printer, when not in use.

In the living room Adeline has combined her love of Scandinavian design and Japanese style effortlessly. A colourful collection of cute cushions brings comfort and texture to every chair in the room, while lots of Adeline's handmade paper creations adorn the home, from garlands and paper flowers to origami birds.

Above A compact space calls for compact furniture and great storage solutions. Here Adeline has opted for petite retro armchairs and created built-in cupboards and shelving almost anywhere she could make it fit. Even the television has been mounted into a recess in the wall, and can be covered with some lengths of fabric when they want to disguise it.

Opposite top Adeline is not afraid of using colour – bright tiles, floral textiles and multicoloured kitchenware all make the space feel cheerful and fun.

ADELINE KLAM
54 Boulevard Richard Lenoir 75011 Paris, France
www.adelineklam.com

100 BEST SHOPS DIRECTORY

LIFESTYLE SHOPS

13, NORWAY
Halfdan Wilhelmsens alle 13
3116 Tønsberg, Norway
www.13tretten.blogspot.co.uk

ALDER AND CO
616 SW 12th Ave. Portland,
OR 97205, United States
www.alderandcoshop.com

ALL THE LUCK IN THE WORLD
Gerard Doustraat 86hs
1072VW Amsterdam, Netherlands
www.alltheluckintheworld.nl

ATOMIC GARDEN
5453 College Ave, Oakland,
CA 94618, United States
www.atomicgardenoakland.com

BONJOUR
31 Mills Street Albert Park
Melbourne, Australia
www.bonjour.com.au

BROOME STREET GENERAL
2912 Rowena Ave, Los Angeles,
CA 90039, United States
www.broomestgeneral.com

BIG AND BELG
Jan Pieter Heijestraat 83,
1053 GM Amsterdam, Netherlands
www.bigenbelg.nl

CARAVAN
5 Ravenscroft Street,
London E2 7SH, UK
www.caravanstyle.com

CRATE EXPECTATIONS
1A Llaneast Street,
Malvern VIC 3144, Australia
www.crateexpectations.com.au

DAILY POETRY
Torenallee 22-02,
5617 Eindhoven, Netherlands
www.daily-poetry.nl

THE FAMILY COMPANY
Shop 4 Ballance Street Village,
Gisborne, New Zealand
www.thefamilycompany.co.nz

FATHER RABBIT
20 Normanby Road, Mt Eden,
Auckland, New Zealand
232 Jervois Road, Herne Bay,
Auckland, New Zealand
www.fatherrabbit.com

GENERAL STORE
1801 Lincoln Blvd, Venice,
CA, United States
www.shop-generalstore.com

THE HAMBLEDON
10 The Square,
Winchester SO23 9ES, UK
www.thehambledon.com

KITSCH KITCHEN
Rozengracht 8-12
1016 NB Amsterdam, Netherlands
www.kitschkitchen.nl

LARK
30 Armstrong St N,
Ballarat VIC 3350, Australia
www.larkstore.com.au

LIV
Lutterothstraße 8,
20255 Hamburg, Germany
www.livhamburg.de

LOWELL
819 N Russell St, Portland,
OR 97227, United States
www.lowellportland.com

NEST
2300 Fillmore St, San Francisco,
CA 94115, United States
www.nestsf.com

OH HELLO FRIEND
122 N. Harbor Blvd, Suite 104/105
Fullerton, California 92832, United States
www.ohhellofriend.com

OLULA
Calle Amaniel, 20,
28015 Madrid, Spain
www.olula-la.blogspot.com.es

THE OTHERIST
Leliegracht 6,
1015 DE Amsterdam, Netherlands
www.otherist.com

PAXTON GATE
824 Valencia Street San Francisco,
CA 94110, United States
4204 N. Mississippi Avenue, Portland,
OR 97217, United States
www.paxtongate.com

THE PEOPLE SHOP
50 Poplar Road, Birmingham,
West Midlands B14 7AG, *UK*
www.thepeopleshop.co.uk

THE PERISH TRUST
728 Divisadero St, San Francisco,
CA 94117, United States
www.theperishtrust.com

PETITE VIOLETTE
Davidshallstorg 1
211 45 Malmö, Sweden
www.shop-en.petiteviolette.com

PETIT PAN
39 Rue François Miron
Paris, France
www.petitpan.com

POKETO
820 E 3rd St, Los Angeles,
CA 90013, United States
www.poketo.com

RARE BIRD
Marnixstraat 127,
1015 VK Amsterdam, Netherlands
www.rarebird.nl

REFORM SCHOOL
3902 Sunset Blvd, Los Angeles,
CA 90029, United States
www.reformschoolrules.com

RE FOUND OBJECTS
Bishops Yard, Main Street , Corbridge,
Northumberland, NE45 5LA, UK
www.re-foundobjects.com

SILO
Senefelderstraße 33,
10437 Berlin, Germany
www.silo-store.com

SIX AND SONS
Haarlemmerdijk 31I,
1013 KA Amsterdam, Netherlands
www.sixandsons.com

SPECIES BY THE THOUSANDS
171 South 4th Street, Williamsburg,
Brooklyn, NY 11211,United States
www.speciesbythethousands.com

SUMMER CAMP
1020 W Ojai Ave, Ojai,
CA 93023, United States
www.hopsummercamp.com

TANTRUM
858 Cole St, San Francisco,
CA 94117, United States
www.shoptantrum.com

TAS-KA
Prins Hendrikstraat 97,
2518 HM Den Haag, Netherlands
www.tas-ka.nl

TING
Rykestraße 41, 10405 Berlin,
Germany
www.ting-shop.com

THE WEBB ST COMPANY
2 Webb Street, Fowey,
Cornwall, PL23 1AP, UK
www.thewebbstreetcompany.co.uk

THE WOODSFOLK
39 Church Street,
Hawthorn VIC 3122, Australia
www.thewoodsfolk.com.au

VINTAGE SHOPS

BAILEYS HOME & GARDEN
Whitecross farm, Bridstow,
Ross-on-wye, Herefordshire,
HR9 6JU, UK
www.baileyshome.com

BEAM & ANCHOR
2710 N Interstate Ave, Portland,
OR 97227, United States
www.beamandanchor.com

BIG DADDY'S ANTIQUES
3334 La Cienega Place, Los Angeles,
CA 90016, United States
1550 17th Street, San Francisco,
CA 94107, United States
bwww.dantiques.com

BILLY GOAT VINTAGE
200 SW Broadway, Portland,
OR 97205, United States
www.billygoatvintageclothing.com

DUSTY DECO
Hornstullstrand 7, Stockholm,
Sweden
www.dustydeco.tictail.com

EMPIRE VINTAGE
63 Cardigan Place, Albert Park,
VIC 3206, Australia
www.empirevintage.com.au

FABRIKEN
Ekedalsgatan 16, 414 66 Gothenburg,
Sweden
www.fabrikengbg.se

FLOTSAM AND JETSAM
84 Ponsonby Road, Ponsonby,
Auckland, New Zealand
www.flotsamandjetsam.co.nz

HARVEST & CO.
Tweede Helmersstraat 90-96,
1054 CM Amsterdam, Netherlands
www.harvestandcompany.com

HOME BARN
Marlow Rd, Little Marlow, Marlow,
Buckinghamshire SL7 3RR, UK
www.homebarnshop.co.uk

INHERITANCE
8055 Beverly Blvd, Los Angeles,
CA 90048, United States
www.inheritanceshop.com

KABINETT AND KAMMER
7 Main Street, Andes,
NY 13731, United States
www.kabinettandkammer.com

L'OBJET QUI PARLE
86 rue des Martyrs
75018 Paris, France

MAVEN COLLECTIVE
7819 SE Stark St,
Portland, OR 97215,
United States
www.mavencollectivepdx.com

PHOENIX ON GOLBRONE
67 Golborne Road,
London W10 5NP, UK
www.phoenixongolborne.co.uk

TOMBEES DU CAMION
17 Rue Joseph de Maistre,
75018 Paris, France
www.tombeesducamion.com

VINTAGE FACTORY
Svandammsvägen 8
126 34 Hägersten, Stockholm, Sweden
www.vintagefabriken.se

WALLFLOWER
1176 Valencia St,
San Francisco, CA 94110, United States
www.shopwallflower.com

HOMEWARE SHOPS

ARTILLERIET
Magasinsgatan 19,
411 18 Gothenburg, Sweden
www.artilleriet.se

BETONNGRUVAN
Sveavägen 133,
113 46 Stockholm, Sweden
www.blogg.betonggruvan.se

BROOKLYN SLATE
305 Van Brunt St, Brooklyn,
NY 11231, United States
www.brooklynslate.com

COLLYERS MANSION
368 Stratford Rd, Brooklyn,
NY 11218, United States
www.shopthemansion.com

DEKOR
2145 Sunset Blvd, Los Angeles,
CA 90026, United States
www.dekorla.com

HENDYS HOME STORE
36 High Street, Hastings
TN34 3ER, UK
www.homestore-hastings.co.uk

HOUSE OF RYM
Hornsgatan 73
118 49 Stockholm, Sweden
www.houseofrym.com

INDUSTRY HOME
740 State St, Santa Barbara,
CA 93101, United States
www.industry-home.com

LABOUR AND WAIT
85 Redchurch Street,
London E2 7DJ, UK
www.labourandwait.co.uk

LOTTA AGATON
Rådmansgatan 7,
114 25 Stockholm, Sweden
www.lottaagaton.se

LUDLOW
7315 Greenwood Ave N,
Seattle, WA 98103, United States
www.ludlowco.com

MAKER AND MOSS
364 Hayes St, San Francisco,
CA 94102, United States
www.makerandmoss.com

NIGHTWOOD
36 Waverly Ave, #326, Brooklyn,
NY 11205, United States
www.nightwoodny.com

OBJECTS OF USE
6 Lincoln House, Market Street,
Oxford OX1 3EQ, UK
www.objectsofuse.com

RARE DEVICE
600 Divisadero St, San Francisco,
CA 94117, United States
4071 24th Street, San Francisco,
CA 94114, United States
www.raredevice.net

RAW MATERIALS
Rozengracht 231,
1016 NA Amsterdam, Netherlands
www.rawmaterials.nl

ROOM TO DREAM
Lenbachplatz 7, 80333 Munich, *Germany*
www.room-to-dream.de

SCOUT
161 Fitzroy Street, St Kilda VIC 3182,
Australia
www.scouthouse.com.au

SHELTER 7
131 Ryrie St, Geelong VIC 3220, Australia
www.shelter7.com.au

STORE WITHOUT A HOME
Haarlemmerdijk 26, 1013 JD Amsterdam,
Netherlands
www.storewithoutahome.nl

SUKHA
Haarlemmerstraat 110,
1013 EW Amsterdam, Netherlands
www.sukha-amsterdam.nl

CAFE SHOPS

BLEND & BLENDER
Hendrik van Viandenstraat 6,
3817 AB Amersfoort, Netherlands
www.blendenblender.nl

CROWN AND CRUMPET
1746 Post St, San Francisco,
CA 94115, United States
www.crownandcrumpet.com

DRINK, SHOP & DO
9 Caledonian Road,
London N1 9DX, UK
www.drinkshopdo.com

HOMECOMING
107 Franklin St, Brooklyn, NY 11222,
United States
www.homecominghome.com

HUTSPOT
Van Woustraat 4, 1073 LL Amsterdam,
Netherlands
www.hutspotamsterdam.com

LATEI
Zeedijk 143, 1012 AW Amsterdam,
Netherlands
www.latei.net

LE ROCKETSHIP
13 Rue Henry Monnier,
75009 Paris, France
www.lerocketship.com

OUTDATED CAFÉ
314 Wall St, Kingston, NY 12401,
United States
www.facebook.com/outdatedcafe

PETERSHAM NURSERIES
Petersham Road, Richmond,
Surrey TW10 7AG, UK
www.petershamnurseries.com

PITFIELD
31-35 Pitfield Street,
London N1 6HB, UK
www.pitfieldlondon.com

STUDIO BOMBA
324 Oxford St, Leederville WA 6007,
Australia
www.studiobomba.com.au

CRAFT SHOPS

ADELINE KLAM
54 Boulevard Richard Lenoir,
75011 Paris, France
www.adelineklam.com

BLACK OVEJA
Calle Sagasta, 7, 28004 Madrid, Spain
www.blackoveja.com

LOOP
15 Camden Passage, Islington,
London N1 8EA, UK
www.loopknitting.com

NADELWALD
Friedelstraße 11,
12047 Berlin, Germany
www.nadelwald.me

THE OLD HABERDASHERY
33 High Street, Ticehurst,
East Sussex TN5 7AS. UK

PURL SOHO
459 Broome St, New York,
NY 10013, United States
www.purlsoho.com

RAW CRAFT
31 Hoddle Street,
Robertson, NSW, Australia
www.rawcraft.net

SEW OVER IT
78 Landor Road,
London SW9 9PH, UK
36A Myddelton Street
London EC1R 1UA. UK
sewoverit.co.uk

STOFF AND CO
Augustenstenstraße 76,
80333 Munich, Germany
www.stoff-and-co.de

TWINKLE TWINKLE
Kollwitzstraße 52,
10405 Berlin, Germany
www.twinkletwinkle.de

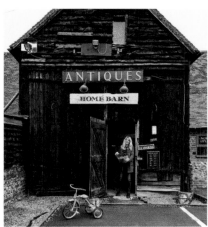

PICTURE CREDITS

Page 1 Jacqui Small LLP/Simon Upton; **2-3** Duncan Innes; **4** Jacqui Small LLP/Michael Sinclair; **7** Sukha; **8-11** Jacqui Small LLP/Simon Upton; **12** Holly Marder; **13** top left Jacqui Small LLP/Simon Upton; **13** top right Jacqui Small LLP/Michael Sinclair; **13** bottom left Jacqui Small LLP/Simon Upton; **13** bottom right Sukha; **14** Jacqui Small LLP/Michael Sinclair; **15** Jacqui Small LLP/Janis Nicolay; **16** Michael Sinclair; **17** left Jacqui Small LLP/Michael Sinclair; **17** right Jacqui Small LLP/Michael Sinclair; **18** Jacqui Small LLP/Janis Nicolay; **19** Jacqui Small LLP/Michael Sinclair; **20-21** Jacqui Small LLP/Simon Upton; **22** Jacqui Small LLP/Janis Nicolay; **23** Sukha; **24** (1, 2) Jacqui Small LLP/Michael Sinclair; **24** (3) Jacqui Small LLP/Janis Nicolay; **24** (4) Jacqui Small LLP/Simon Upton; **24** (5) Jacqui Small LLP/Nick Carter; **24** (6) Jacqui Small LLP/Janis Nicolay; **24** (7) Jacqui Small LLP/Simon Upton; **24** (8) Jacqui Small LLP/Nick Carter; **24** (9) Sukha; **24** (10) Jacqui Small LLP/Janis Nicolay; **26** Sukha; **27** top left Jacqui Small LLP/Janis Nicolay; **27** top right Jacqui Small LLP/Michael Sinclair; **27** bottom Jacqui Small LLP/Janis Nicolay; **28** left Jacqui Small LLP/Michael Sinclair; **28** right Jacqui Small LLP/Janis Nicolay; **29** above and below Jacqui Small LLP/Michael Sinclair; **30** Jacqui Small LLP/Simon Upton; **31** Mikkel Vang/Taverne Agency; **32** Jacqui Small LLP/Michael Sinclair **33** Jacqui Small LLP/Janis Nicolay; **34** Jacqui Small LLP/Janis Nicolay; **35** Jacqui Small LLP/Michael Sinclair; **36-37** Sukha; **38-39** Jacqui Small LLP/Michael Sinclair; **40-41** Jacqui Small LLP/Janis Nicolay; **42** Jacqui Small LLP/Michael Sinclair; **43** Jacqui Small LLP/Nick Carter (top) Jacqui Small LLP/Janis Nicolay (bottom) OHF; **44** Jacqui Small LLP/Michael Sinclair; **45** Jacqui Small LLP/Janis Nicolay; **46** Jacqui Small LLP/Michael Sinclair; **47** Jacqui Small LLP/Janis Nicolay; **48** Jacqui Small LLP/Janis Nicolay; **49** above Jacqui Small LLP/Simon Upton; **49** below Jacqui Small LLP/Janis Nicolay; **50** (1) Jacqui Small LLP/Michael Sinclair; **50** (2) Jacqui Small LLP/Janis Nicolay; **50** (3 and 4) Jacqui Small LLP/Michael Sinclair; **50** (5) Jacqui Small LLP/Janis Nicolay; **50** (6) Jacqui Small LLP/Janis Nicolay; **50** (7) Holly Marder; **50** (8 and 9) Jacqui Small LLP/Simon Upton; **50** (10) Jacqui Small LLP/Michael Sinclair; **52** Jacqui Small LLP/Janis Nicolay; **53** Lauren Bamford; **54-55** Mikkel Vang/Taverne Agency; **56** Jacqui Small LLP/Michael Sinclair; **57** above left Jacqui Small LLP/Michael Sinclair; **57** above right Jacqui Small LLP/Michael Sinclair; **57** below left Jacqui Small LLP/Simon Upton; **57** below right Jacqui Small LLP/Janis Nicolay; **58-59** Mikkel Vang/Taverne Agency; **60-61** Mikkel Vang/Taverne Agency **62** top left Jacqui Small LLP/Janis Nicolay; **62** top centre Jacqui Small LLP/Nick Carter; **62** top right Jacqui Small LLP/Janis Nicolay; **62** middle left Jacqui Small LLP/Janis Nicolay; **62** middle centre Jacqui Small LLP/Janis Nicolay;**62** middle right Jacqui Small LLP/Janis Nicolay; **62** bottom left Jacqui Small LLP/Janis Nicolay; **62** bottom centre Jacqui Small LLP/Janis Nicolay; **62** bottom right Jacqui Small LLP/Janis Nicolay; **65-73** Jacqui Small LLP/Janis Nicolay; **74-77** Duncan Innes; **78-79** Duncan Innes/Homestyle magazine; **80-95** Jacqui Small LLP/Janis Nicolay; **96-101** Michael Sinclair; **102-107** Jacqui Small LLP/Michael Sinclair; **108** top left Jacqui Small LLP/Janis Nicolay; **108** top centre Jacqui Small LLP/Janis Nicolay; **108** top right Holly Marder ; **108** middle left Jacqui Small LLP/Janis Nicolay; **108** middle centre Jacqui Small LLP/Simon Upton; **108** middle right Holly Marder **107** bottom left Holly Marder; **107** bottom centre Jacqui Small LLP/Simon Upton; **107** bottom right Jacqui Small LLP/Nick Carter; **111** Jacqui Small LLP/Nick Carter; **112-119** Jacqui Small LLP/Simon Upton; **120-125** Jacqui Small LLP/Janis Nicolay; **126-133** Michael Sinclair; **134-137** Jacqui Small LLP/Simon Upton; **138-139** Lauren Bamford; **140-141** Mikkel Vang/Taverne Agency; **142-145** Jacqui Small LLP/Nick Carter; **146-153** Jacqui Small LLP/Janis Nicolay; **154** top left Jacqui Small LLP/Janis Nicolay; **154** top centre Jacqui Small LLP/Nick Carter; **154** top right Jacqui Small LLP/Janis Nicolay; **154** middle left Jacqui Small LLP/Simon Upton; **154** middle centre Jacqui Small LLP/Janis Nicolay; **154** middle right Jacqui Small LLP/Simon Upton; **154** bottom left Jacqui Small LLP/Nick Carter; **154** bottom centre Jacqui Small LLP/Simon Upton; **154** bottom right Jacqui Small LLP/Janis Nicolay; **157-163** Jacqui Small LLP/Simon Upton; **164-167** Jacqui Small LLP/Nick Carter **168-173** Jacqui Small LLP/Janis Nicolay; **174** top left Jacqui Small LLP/Nick Carter; **174** top centre Jacqui Small LLP/Simon Upton; **174** top right Jacqui Small LLP/Nick Carter; **174** middle left Jacqui Small LLP/Nick Carter; **174** middle centre Jacqui Small LLP/Nick Carter; **174** middle right Jacqui Small LLP/Nick Carter; **174** bottom left Jacqui Small LLP/Simon Upton; **174** bottom centre Jacqui Small LLP/Nick Carter; **174** bottom right Jacqui Small LLP/Nick Carter; **177** Jacqui Small LLP/Nick Carter; **178-183** Jacqui Small LLP/Simon Upton; **184-193** Jacqui Small LLP/Nick Carter; **194** top left and top centre Jacqui Small LLP/Michael Sinclair; **194** top right Jacqui Small LLP/Simon Upton; **194** middle left Jacqui Small LLP/Michael Sinclair; **194** middle centre Jacqui Small LLP/Simon Upton; **194** middle right Jacqui Small LLP/Michael Sinclair; **194** bottom left Jacqui Small LLP/Simon Upton; **194** bottom centre Jacqui Small LLP/Michael Sinclair; **194** bottom right Jacqui Small LLP/Simon Upton; **199-207** Jacqui Small LLP/Michael Sinclair; **208-213** Jacqui Small LLP/Simon Upton; **214-217** Jacqui Small LLP/Michael Sinclair; **218-221** Jacqui Small LLP/Simon Upton

AUTHOR'S ACKNOWLEDGEMENTS

The journey of making this book ran parallel to the life-changing event of me becoming a mother. Ruby came into the world the week we started shooting the first photography, and has been by my side ever since as I've juggled these two very new experiences. I hope one day when she sees this book she will be inspired to always follow her dreams no matter what, just like her mum has done.

Thank you to Jacqui Small for making this dream come true for me and for believing in my idea. I've loved every moment of working with the wonderful team. Thank you Jo Copestick, for your guidance with tackling the mammoth task

of writing the words and thank you Rachel Cross, for your fabulous design skills, patience and late night emails!

I've been lucky enough to work with four fabulous photographers on this book – all of whom I couldn't be more grateful to for producing such stunning images. Thank you so much Michael Sinclair, Nick Carter, Janis Nicolay and Simon Upton – all super-talented and super-lovely people.

A huge thank you to each and every shopkeeper whose shops and homes are featured within these pages. What you do inspires me so much.

Finally, thank you to my parents who regularly made the trip from Belfast to

London, to look after Ruby while I worked on the book, and for letting me follow my dream to London all those years ago. And last but definitely not least – thank you to my amazing husband Simon, for always supporting me in my crazy creative plans. Love you more. x